Pearson
PUBLISHING

Student Handbook
Key Skills:
Communication

Nick Kiernan

Cartoons by Steve Clarke

Name: ....

Class: ....

School: ....

....

Exam board: ....

Specification number: ....

Candidate number: ....

Centre number: ....

Further copies of this publication may be obtained from:

Pearson Publishing
Chesterton Mill, French's Road, Cambridge CB4 3NP
Tel 01223 350555 Fax 01223 356484

Email info@pearson.co.uk
Web site www.pearsonpublishing.co.uk

ISBN: 1 85749 702 3

Published by Pearson Publishing 2001
© Pearson Publishing 2001

We are grateful to the QCA for allowing us to reproduce the sample examinations on
pages 89 to 98 and pages 104 to 111, and the glossary on pages 112 to 114.

Contents

Introduction

Everyone's experience of education is different. However, there are a number of valuable skills that underpin our education. These should help us through all areas of our education and future learning in college, at university, at work or in our own time.

What are the Key Skills?

Key Skills are:

- **general skills** used to improve your learning and performance. They are needed in education, work and everyday life

- **essential in education** because they help you to demonstrate and communicate your ideas and knowledge

- **essential in employment** – if you have Key Skills certificates, an employer will feel confident about your ability in specific areas, eg literacy. Most people will have several jobs during their lifetime; Key Skills are essential to help you to adapt to different types of job and to remain employable during your working life

- **essential in everyday life** because they are the skills you will need repeatedly. You will need to talk to others, write letters, understand information given in newspapers, books, etc.

The Key Skills qualification was made available from September 2000 and is designed to allow students to demonstrate and improve their proficiency in up to six different areas. The three core Key Skills are:

- Communication
- Application of Number
- Information Technology.

Together these make up the Key Skills qualification. The three wider Key Skills are:

- Working with Others
- Improving own Learning and Performance
- Problem Solving.

The first three Key Skills are available at different levels (1 to 5), with each successive level representing a progression from the one before. The last three Key Skills are available from Levels 1 to 3.

Key Skills may be obtained through the study of NVQs, GNVQs, GCE AS/A-levels or the International Baccalaureate. This handbook is concerned with the Communication Key Skill at Level 3. Although explanation for Levels 1 and 2 has been provided for background information, you should aim to achieve Level 3.

Obtaining your certificates

In order to secure this qualification, you need to provide evidence, either through specially designated tasks or through tasks in courses you are already studying. This evidence should then be collected in a clearly indexed portfolio. There will be an internal assessment of your portfolio. It will be assessed by your teachers and verified (checked) by the examination board. When your portfolio material reaches a satisfactory standard, it will be signed off by the Standards Moderator (external examiner) and you will receive a Unit Certificate.

You will also need to pass an externally-verified examination, lasting 90 minutes. This is called an External Assessment Instrument (EAI). When you pass an EAI, you receive a Test Certificate.

Using this handbook

This handbook provides advice on:

- developing the necessary skills
- gathering evidence for your portfolio
- passing the examination.

A glossary of terms used in Key Skills specifications can be found on pages 112 to 114.

Copies of the tracking calendars (pages viii to xi) and planning sheets (pages 42 to 49) used within the handbook are also available on our Web site at http://www.pearsonpublishing.co.uk/publications/extras/.

'Now what?'

Planning your approach

Many post-16 courses are divided into two sections. For example, you can study an AS-level in Year 12 and then the A-level in Year 13. It is advisable to try and complete most of your Key Skills work in Year 12 as this will allow you more time to concentrate on A-levels in Year 13. It is therefore a good idea to begin collecting evidence for your Key Skills portfolio as soon as possible in Year 12. It may also help you to adjust to the new demands of post-16 courses as you will need to focus on skills that will be very useful to help you through your main courses.

*'The evidence is in there **somewhere**...'*

The externally-assessed Key Skills Communication examination can be taken at a number of points throughout the year and can be retaken as many times as necessary. You will need to discuss the best time for you to take the exam with your assessor.

If you are confident that you have mastered the skills to the required level then you will benefit from taking the exam at the earliest opportunity. You should also be able to gather the required evidence fairly quickly. This will then allow you to concentrate on your core studies. If you need time to develop the skills then you will evidently benefit from delaying taking the exam until you have been able to practise them. You may need several attempts at, for example, giving a presentation, before you feel confident and can present evidence of the required standard.

Tracking calendars

It is important to keep a clear record of your Key Skills progress. The tracking calendars on pages ix to xi allow you to keep a record of the assignments for each element of the Communication Key Skill, as well as any exam preparation you may wish to do.

To use the tracking calendars, choose a different colour for each of the headings in the key below and fill in the boxes beside them. (If you wish to record other dates or deadlines, etc, you can add them to the key in the spaces provided.) Use the key to colour in the relevant sections of the appropriate tracking calendar. You will then be able to see at a glance when you have to complete your Key Skills work.

Key

Assignment deadlines ☐
Exam preparation ☐
Mock exam dates ☐
Dates of exam ☐
.... ☐
.... ☐
.... ☐
.... ☐

Tracking calendar 2001-2002

	S	S	M	T	W	T	F	S	S	M	T	W	T	F	S	S	M	T	W	T	F	S	S	M	T	W	T	F	S	S	M	T	W	T	F	S	S
SEP	1	2	3	4	5	6	7	8	9	10	11	12	13	14	15	16	17	18	19	20	21	22	23	24	25	26	27	28	29	30							
OCT			1	2	3	4	5	6	7	8	9	10	11	12	13	14	15	16	17	18	19	20	21	22	23	24	25	26	27	28	29	30	31				
NOV						1	2	3	4	5	6	7	8	9	10	11	12	13	14	15	16	17	18	19	20	21	22	23	24	25	26	27	28	29	30		
DEC	1	2	3	4	5	6	7	8	9	10	11	12	13	14	15	16	17	18	19	20	21	22	23	24	25	26	27	28	29	30	31						
JAN				1	2	3	4	5	6	7	8	9	10	11	12	13	14	15	16	17	18	19	20	21	22	23	24	25	26	27	28	29	30	31			
FEB							1	2	3	4	5	6	7	8	9	10	11	12	13	14	15	16	17	18	19	20	21	22	23	24	25	26	27	28			
MAR							1	2	3	4	5	6	7	8	9	10	11	12	13	14	15	16	17	18	19	20	21	22	23	24	25	26	27	28	29	30	31
APR			1	2	3	4	5	6	7	8	9	10	11	12	13	14	15	16	17	18	19	20	21	22	23	24	25	26	27	28	29	30					
MAY					1	2	3	4	5	6	7	8	9	10	11	12	13	14	15	16	17	18	19	20	21	22	23	24	25	26	27	28	29	30	31		
JUN	1	2	3	4	5	6	7	8	9	10	11	12	13	14	15	16	17	18	19	20	21	22	23	24	25	26	27	28	29	30							
JUL			1	2	3	4	5	6	7	8	9	10	11	12	13	14	15	16	17	18	19	20	21	22	23	24	25	26	27	28	29	30	31				
AUG						1	2	3	4	5	6	7	8	9	10	11	12	13	14	15	16	17	18	19	20	21	22	23	24	25	26	27	28	29	30	31	

Tracking calendar 2002-2003

Month	S	S	M	T	W	T	F	S	S	M	T	W	T	F	S	S	M	T	W	T	F	S	S	M	T	W	T	F	S	S	M	T	W	T	F	S	S	M
SEP		1	2	3	4	5	6	7	8	9	10	11	12	13	14	15	16	17	18	19	20	21	22	23	24	25	26	27	28	29	30							
OCT				1	2	3	4	5	6	7	8	9	10	11	12	13	14	15	16	17	18	19	20	21	22	23	24	25	26	27	28	29	30	31				
NOV							1	2	3	4	5	6	7	8	9	10	11	12	13	14	15	16	17	18	19	20	21	22	23	24	25	26	27	28	29	30		
DEC		1	2	3	4	5	6	7	8	9	10	11	12	13	14	15	16	17	18	19	20	21	22	23	24	25	26	27	28	29	30	31						
JAN					1	2	3	4	5	6	7	8	9	10	11	12	13	14	15	16	17	18	19	20	21	22	23	24	25	26	27	28	29	30	31			
FEB								1	2	3	4	5	6	7	8	9	10	11	12	13	14	15	16	17	18	19	20	21	22	23	24	25	26	27	28			
MAR								1	2	3	4	5	6	7	8	9	10	11	12	13	14	15	16	17	18	19	20	21	22	23	24	25	26	27	28	29	30	31
APR				1	2	3	4	5	6	7	8	9	10	11	12	13	14	15	16	17	18	19	20	21	22	23	24	25	26	27	28	29	30					
MAY						1	2	3	4	5	6	7	8	9	10	11	12	13	14	15	16	17	18	19	20	21	22	23	24	25	26	27	28	29	30	31		
JUN		1	2	3	4	5	6	7	8	9	10	11	12	13	14	15	16	17	18	19	20	21	22	23	24	25	26	27	28	29	30							
JUL				1	2	3	4	5	6	7	8	9	10	11	12	13	14	15	16	17	18	19	20	21	22	23	24	25	26	27	28	29	30	31				
AUG							1	2	3	4	5	6	7	8	9	10	11	12	13	14	15	16	17	18	19	20	21	22	23	24	25	26	27	28	29	30	31	

x

Tracking calendar 2003-2004

Month	S	M	T	W	T	F	S
SEP		1	2	3	4	5	6
	7	8	9	10	11	12	13
	14	15	16	17	18	19	20
	21	22	23	24	25	26	27
	28	29	30				
OCT				1	2	3	4
	5	6	7	8	9	10	11
	12	13	14	15	16	17	18
	19	20	21	22	23	24	25
	26	27	28	29	30	31	
NOV							1
	2	3	4	5	6	7	8
	9	10	11	12	13	14	15
	16	17	18	19	20	21	22
	23	24	25	26	27	28	29
	30						
DEC		1	2	3	4	5	6
	7	8	9	10	11	12	13
	14	15	16	17	18	19	20
	21	22	23	24	25	26	27
	28	29	30	31			
JAN					1	2	3
	4	5	6	7	8	9	10
	11	12	13	14	15	16	17
	18	19	20	21	22	23	24
	25	26	27	28	29	30	31
FEB	1	2	3	4	5	6	7
	8	9	10	11	12	13	14
	15	16	17	18	19	20	21
	22	23	24	25	26	27	28
	29						
MAR		1	2	3	4	5	6
	7	8	9	10	11	12	13
	14	15	16	17	18	19	20
	21	22	23	24	25	26	27
	28	29	30	31			
APR					1	2	3
	4	5	6	7	8	9	10
	11	12	13	14	15	16	17
	18	19	20	21	22	23	24
	25	26	27	28	29	30	
MAY							1
	2	3	4	5	6	7	8
	9	10	11	12	13	14	15
	16	17	18	19	20	21	22
	23	24	25	26	27	28	29
	30	31					
JUN			1	2	3	4	5
	6	7	8	9	10	11	12
	13	14	15	16	17	18	19
	20	21	22	23	24	25	26
	27	28	29	30			
JUL					1	2	3
	4	5	6	7	8	9	10
	11	12	13	14	15	16	17
	18	19	20	21	22	23	24
	25	26	27	28	29	30	31
AUG	1	2	3	4	5	6	7
	8	9	10	11	12	13	14
	15	16	17	18	19	20	21
	22	23	24	25	26	27	28
	29	30	31				

Part 1

The skills

What are the skills?

There are four main skill areas which are assessed in Key Skills Communication. These are:

- Discussion
- Presentation
- Reading
- Writing.

These skills can be considered separately, but will frequently overlap. For example, reading skills are often essential preparation for writing, discussion or presentation skills.

You should already have a lot of experience of all these skills since reading, writing, and speaking and listening form the main blocks of English teaching in schools and colleges. The Key Skills Communication qualification seeks to develop these skills and provide a solid base for any future activities.

'So... what am I looking for?'

Discussion

Discussion skills are very important in many areas of education, business and leisure. The ability to brainstorm ideas with others, express criticisms and objections, offer support and encouragement can make a big difference to your understanding of different subjects and to your ability to work as a team.

Individuals benefit from good discussion skills because they can put their views across to others convincingly. **Groups** benefit from good discussion skills because more people can contribute ideas and opinions in a focused, efficient and effective manner.

A discussion can be defined as a conversation between at least two people that attempts to achieve a common goal.

Good discussion skills at all levels require you to be aware of who you are in discussion with (the **audience**) and why you are having the discussion (the **purpose**).

The following pages are designed to show you what you need to know to achieve Level 3 in discussion. They provide help in developing these skills and suggest ways of accumulating evidence of these skills. Each level is designed to build on the previous one so explanations for Levels 1 and 2 have also been provided.

*'So... **why** are we having this discussion?'*

Level 1

To achieve Level 1, you should be able to do the following.

Find out about the subject so you can say things that are relevant

You need to find out what the subject is and understand the purpose of the discussion. Decide what you think about the subject and why you have these opinions. For example, if you are going to discuss whether footballers are paid too much, it would be worth finding out how much a range of different players are paid, how much players were paid in the past and how their salaries compare to other jobs.

Judge when to speak and how much to say

A successful discussion involves some input from everyone who is present. This means that you need to practise taking turns to speak. If you want to make a particular point, you need to judge when it is best to make it. This is easier if there is an agenda of things to be discussed, but you may have to create your own opening to speak. Useful phrases include:

- I would like to draw everyone's attention to...
- If I could move on from the last point to...
- I feel this might be a good time to mention...

She was beginning to wonder if maybe she had gone on long enough...

You also need to judge how long it is appropriate to speak for. Consider the following:

- How relevant your point is to the main topic of the discussion.
- How long the discussion is scheduled to last for.
- How many other people are involved in the discussion.

Say things that suit the purpose of the discussion

You need to practise contributing to discussions in a variety of ways. Different purposes require different skills and approaches. For example, explaining something at the start of a discussion may require more detail than offering an opinion or asking questions. Similarly, providing information for others requires a different style of language to finding out information from the discussion leader.

Speak clearly in a way that suits the situation

Be aware that different types of discussion require you to adapt the way you present yourself. For example, a discussion with your friends is different to a discussion with employers or teachers because it is less formal. Experiment with varying the following to make your contributions appropriate to your discussion:

- The **volume** at which you speak – This will be affected by the size of the discussion group and also by the people you are with. It may be inappropriate to raise your voice in some circumstances but be more suitable in others.

*It was a fine line between loud and **too** loud!*

- The **speed** at which you speak – If people are depending on you to provide clear information then you should concentrate on talking more slowly than normal so that everyone can follow you.

- The **level of formality** – People you are familiar with will be more tolerant of, for example, slang, than people who do not know you.

- The amount of **specialist language** or **jargon** that you use – If your audience does not know as much about a subject as you, try to avoid using terms they may not understand. Alternatively, you may need to explain new terms at the beginning. This should be done as clearly as possible.

Show you are listening closely to what others say

You should use body language to show you are paying attention. For example, sitting forward and looking at the person who is speaking rather than slumping back and staring out of the window. You can also encourage or support other people's contributions, for example, by asking questions that show you have been paying attention, or by agreeing with them as they make their points.

His was not a body that readily supported 'dynamic' presentations

Level 2

To achieve Level 2, you should be able to do the following.

Use varied vocabulary and expressions to suit your purpose
You should try to think carefully about the points you want to make and how to put them across. Try not to repeat yourself or stray off the subject as this will lose your audience's interest.

Adapt your contributions to suit different situations
As with Level 1, you can vary the speed, volume, level of formality and the amount of detail or jargon you decide to include.

Show you are listening closely and respond appropriately
Again, this closely follows the demands made at Level 1. You should use body language and relevant spoken responses to help bring other people into the discussion.

Identify the speaker's intentions
It is important in all forms of communication to try and establish why someone is either talking or writing to you. For example, in an advertisement it is usually obvious that the advert creators want to persuade us to buy a product or change our behaviour (eg by not drinking and driving). In other situations, the intention may not be as clear. In discussions, someone who appears to be providing helpful information may actually be attempting to persuade us to agree or disagree with their point of view.

Listen carefully to the words different people use and the way they address others to try and work out what they want to achieve in a discussion.

Different intentions include:

- persuading others to agree or disagree with a certain point of view
- making a new idea known
- making a criticism.

'So... what are you hoping to achieve in this discussion?'

Move the discussion forward

This is a difficult skill, but it is important to master it so that your discussions can be successful. Discussions can easily drift away from their main point; therefore, you need to be able to recognise when this is happening and to know how to rectify the situation. Ways to do this include:

- Summarising the most important points that have already been made. This helps everyone to understand what has been said so far and to think about where the discussion could go next.

- Identifying what you think the most important point is and highlighting it so that the discussion follows the direction you want.
- Reminding everyone what the overall purpose of the discussion is in order to bring it back into focus.

This skill can demonstrate your ability to lead a discussion. It maximises the chances of making the points you want and allows people the opportunity to speak about subjects you want to discuss.

Level 3

To achieve Level 3, you should be able to do the following.

Vary how and when you participate to suit your purpose and the situation

This builds on the skills required at Levels 1 and 2, but requires you to be more aware of the nature of the discussion so that you can adapt your contribution. For example, a discussion that develops into an argument with strongly-held opinions may require you to increase the force with which you present your points. Alternatively, you may judge that it is better to listen to what others say and make more general points until you are clear about which side you agree with.

Listen and respond sensitively and develop points and ideas

In addition to the skills mentioned at Levels 1 and 2, you need to think about the people involved in your discussion. You may need to adapt your contributions depending on the different genders, cultural backgrounds or experiences of the people involved. For example, making generalised or uninformed comments that refer to the race or religion of other people in the discussion could easily cause offence and so be inappropriate – as could sexist remarks or assumptions.

As discussions are often built around opposing points of view or controversial subjects, some areas need to be approached maturely and with sensitivity. For example, if the topic was birth control and you know that one of the participants had had an abortion then it would be wise to divert the discussion until you know their feelings on the subject.

Make openings to encourage others to contribute

This again is a skill that requires you to view the other people in your discussion as individuals. It is natural for some people to be more confident and have more to say than others. However, a successful discussion is one where **everyone** is able to contribute. You should be aware who has been dominating the discussion and try to encourage the more reticent people to participate. You can do this by:

- directly inviting people to contribute
- asking questions to draw out points from a range of people
- asking the more assertive people to listen to what others have to say before responding.

Presentation

In order to achieve Levels 2 and 3 (Level 1 is not covered in this skill), it is necessary to give a short talk or presentation. Some people quite naturally find this a daunting task, but it is a useful skill to master. Many jobs revolve around the need for people to present information and ideas to others in person. In order to achieve the Key Skills Communication qualification, you do not have to address a large audience. However, you do need to demonstrate a range of skills that will help you deliver a talk or presentation to a small group on a topic of your choice.

Many people find the idea of speaking in front of others off-putting because they do not like being the centre of attention. This is emphasised in a formal situation where you may feel that any mistake will instantly be noticed and criticised. The best way to overcome these worries is to prepare thoroughly both the content of your talk and the methods you can use to communicate your ideas.

Level 2

To achieve Level 2, you should be able to do the following.

Prepare for the talk

This is probably the most important element because you need to know what you are talking about. It means researching the subject matter by using one or more of the following sources:

- a library
- reference books
- the Internet
- asking people questions
- using a questionnaire.

You should, of course, think about your own ideas, opinions and experiences.

The more information you have, the easier it is to select the parts that will allow you to speak confidently and knowledgeably about your subject, either using notes or from memory.

Adapt your language to suit your subject, purpose and situation

It is very easy to lose interest when someone is talking to you as a member of a group. To avoid this, you should acquire the following skills:

- **Speaking clearly** – This means loudly enough for everyone to hear and using concise sentences that people can follow easily.
- **Avoiding jargon** – If you need to include technical terms, make sure you explain what they mean.
- **Varying the tone of your voice** – If you listen to people speaking on the television or radio, you will notice that they do not speak in one flat tone. They vary the way they speak to keep our attention. For example, questions are spoken in a different way to statements.

- **Varying the speed at which you speak** – As a general rule, you should speak more slowly and deliberately when addressing a group of people to allow them to take in what you are saying.

- **Varying the volume at which you speak** – Some points may be put across most successfully in a strong, assertive manner, whilst, at other times, a quieter, more intimate approach may be more appropriate.

*'Strong and assertive' was **one** thing, but jumping the queue was **another**...*

Structure what you say to help listeners follow a line of thought or series of events

The order in which you present your points is very important. There are several things to consider when planning the sequence of your talk.

Firstly, you need to decide where to start. It may be a good idea to start with a particularly interesting point, fact, statistic, or example in order to catch your audience's attention.

Secondly, you need to explain what you will be talking about and indicate the main points you are going to make. Again, this makes it much easier for your audience to follow what you are saying.

Try to decide on a logical sequence for your ideas. For example, if you are talking about a company's performance over the last year, it would seem logical to follow a description of recent results with hopes and predictions for future performance, based on those results. This may be followed by a suggestion of future changes. Try to create a flow to your talk that will not leave the audience wondering what you will be speaking about next.

Lastly, you need to end on a definite note. You can do this by summarising your main points and repeating the most important idea that you want your audience to remember.

Use images to help others understand the main points of your talk

One of the most common tasks in primary schools is for pupils to bring an item from home in to school and then 'show and tell'. This principle is equally useful in later life. If you are talking to an audience, it is likely that they will be able to see as well as hear you. This means that you can use a variety of visual aids to improve your talk. These help the audience to remain focused on what you have to say by appealing to more than just their sense of hearing.

The 'show and tell' discussion on operational scars
was rapidly getting out of control...

You can use a variety of images in your talk. For example:

- an object, eg a product you have helped produce
- a picture or photograph
- a graph or diagram
- some video footage.

As well as televisions, you can also use overhead projectors or computer equipment to illustrate your talk.

Level 3

To achieve Level 3, you should be able to do the following.

Prepare the presentation to suit your purpose

You need to be clear about why you are giving the presentation. For example, if you are presenting an argument in a debate, you should gather evidence that supports what you are saying and helps persuade others of the validity of your argument. You may also need to try and find evidence that weakens the opposing argument.

If you are presenting findings from an investigation or piece of research, you should gather a different selection of material. It is important to have your intentions, method and results easily available.

Match your language and style to suit the complexity of the subject, the formality of the situation and the needs of the audience

Consider your audience and think about what they are hoping to gain from your talk. It is important to judge how formal you need to be, ie whether it is appropriate to use any slang and jokes. Some audiences will simply want you to communicate your information as succinctly as possible. Other audiences may appreciate your efforts to make your talk entertaining or memorable. The amount of technical language you use should be determined by the knowledge of your audience. If you are talking to fellow experts then you can talk confidently using jargon and assume they can understand you. If you are explaining something new to people then you should spend more time explaining important terms and ideas to them.

You should also consider what the audience will do as a result of your talk. If you expect them to use the information to produce something themselves or to pass it on to other people then your language and style should match their expectations.

Structure what you say
As with Level 2, it is extremely important that you present your points clearly. You should provide 'signposts' for your audience by way of an **introduction**, clear **links** between sections and a definite **ending**.

Try comparing your presentation with a television documentary series. Divide it into clearly-defined sections and think of each one as a separate episode. At the start of episode 1, you would explain what the whole series is about and what each episode will cover. At the end of episode 1, you would briefly sum up what it included and then provide a link which informs the audience what to expect when they tune in for episode 2.

This process of signposting and summing up would continue through the entire series until the end of the final episode when you would briefly pull out the main points that have been made. You should apply the same ideas to your presentation so that your audience can easily follow what you have to say.

Use techniques to engage the audience, including images

These ideas follow on closely from the skills at Level 2 and again require you to consider the needs and expectations of your audience carefully.

It is important that you try to vary the delivery of your presentation both in the way you speak and in the visual aids you choose to employ. You need to think about varying the volume and tone of your voice and the speed at which you speak. You should also utilise visual aids, eg pictures, models, plans, graphs, tables, video, overhead projections, Microsoft® PowerPoint presentations, etc, to help your audience understand the points you are making.

It is also a good idea to give out examples to illustrate what you are saying when appropriate.

He got the distinct impression that his audience was pleased so far...

Reading

From the earliest civilisations to the latest technology, the main way of accessing recorded information has been through reading. Most people have developed a range of reading skills during their time at school (many of which they are unaware of mastering). Reading at different levels involves more than simply decoding letters on the page. You navigate texts by using indexes, reference sections or by looking for headings and keywords. Reading also involves identifying writers' intentions, purposes, and opinions, and following often complex narratives or arguments. Reading in order to obtain, summarise or synthesise information allows you to research talks and discussions as well as informing your own writing and production of documents. This kind of reading skill thus supports the Communication Key Skill in other areas.

Reading at different levels was not always comfortable...

Level 1

To achieve Level 1, you should be able to do the following.

Obtain advice from others on what to read for different purposes

You should be aware that you can read texts for different reasons. For example, you may be reading to:

- find out facts
- establish the different opinions that people hold on a given subject
- find out how to do something
- help you come up with your own ideas on a subject.

Identify the main points and ideas in different types of straightforward material, including images

This means practising reading a range of different texts, eg letters, books, magazines, newspapers, and identifying the most important points that are being made. For example, a newspaper article may contain lots of background information, but its main purpose is to tell us what has happened.

You should also be able to look at pictures, diagrams, charts, maps, etc to establish what they are illustrating.

Use a dictionary

Using a dictionary to check the meanings and correct spellings of words is an essential skill and a good habit for anyone who is trying to read and write accurately.

*There are all **sorts** of words in here...*

Ask others when you are unclear about what you have read

It is often important for several people to reach the same conclusions about what they have read. Therefore, if you are in any doubt about what you have read, do not hesitate to ask questions about the content or meaning.

Prepare information so it is suitable for use

You should be able to make notes on and then organise the information you have found so you can use them in discussion or as the basis for a talk or piece of writing. When you make notes, it is helpful to use headings to group together information that is linked. For example, if you were finding out about employment in Europe, it would be sensible to group information together using different countries as headings.

Notes are most successful when you use bullet points and short phrases rather than long sentences.

It is worth reading to the end of an article or a chapter before you start to make notes. This will help you gain a better understanding of the points that are being made.

The bullet points were simple, but effective...

Level 2

To achieve Level 2, you should be able to do the following.

Use different sources to obtain relevant information

You may be able to find relevant information from more than one place. Using different sources will help you build up a more complete picture of the subject you are researching. For example, if you were trying to find out about an event in history, you could find accounts that contain not only different opinions on past events, but also different selections of facts. One writer or group may not want to mention things that make them sound responsible for a disaster or starting a war, whilst another group may be very keen to include these details.

Alternatively, when seeking information on how to do something, it is worth finding out more than one method and comparing them to find the most appropriate for you.

Skim materials to gain a general idea of content and scan text to identify the information you need from straightforward, extended (more than three A4 pages) documents

You should master the skill of looking quickly at texts for signposts that indicate whether they will be useful or not. For example, titles, headings and subheadings, keywords, pictures and diagrams often provide good clues.

Recognise the writer's intentions

You should look carefully at texts to see if you can tell what their purpose is. They may be designed to provide facts and information, or they may be trying to educate or persuade the reader to agree with a certain point of view.

You can begin to identify a writer's intentions if you look at the headings and pictures; are they trying to put across a certain viewpoint? You should also be aware of phrases that attract your attention in the text. Ask yourself what they make you think and whether they have been used deliberately. For example, a murder case could be described as a 'tragic accident' if the writer believed the suspect was innocent. Alternatively, it could be described as 'cold-blooded slaughter' if the writer believed the suspect was guilty.

It just seemed to reach right out and grab you...

Identify the main lines of reasoning

In the same way that your talks need a clear structure to put across an argument or point of view successfully, so do the things you read. Look for examples where the writer has provided a piece of information or evidence and then drawn a conclusion from it. Words such as 'therefore', 'so' or 'whereas' often signal this kind of writing is taking place:

The conditions in Germany during the 1930s were very harsh; **therefore**, *it made people more willing to accept the extreme ideas of the Nazis as possible solutions to their problems.*

Summarise information for a purpose

It is important that you are aware of the purpose of your reading before you begin. This is because you will not want to waste time ploughing through lots of material and making notes on information that is not directly relevant to you. If you are going to use the information to prepare for a talk or report then it will be worthwhile deciding on a rough version of what you want to say before you begin reading. You can then use your research to build up your knowledge of these areas and expand into new areas.

Level 3

To achieve Level 3, you should be able to do the following.

Find and skim read extended (more than three A4 pages) documents, such as textbooks, secondary sources, articles and reports, to identify relevant material

As with Levels 1 and 2, it is useful to be able to look rapidly through potential sources of reference and use headings, pictures, indexes, keywords, titles and subtitles, Internet search engines, bookmarks, etc to navigate your way to and around relevant texts and sections of text. This enables you to extend your knowledge around a subject and also to accumulate alternative and supplementary viewpoints, opinions, ideas and evidence.

Scan and read the material to find the specific information you need

This skill is a more precise version of the previous one. Avoid reading irrelevant material so use textual signposts (headings, indexes, keywords, tables, diagrams, pictures, etc) to navigate your way around the text and to find the information that you want.

Use appropriate sources of reference to help you understand complex lines of reasoning and information from text and images

This requires you to use more than one source of information so you can build up a fuller picture of the subject you are researching. It is helpful to learn about alternative accounts, methods, opinions and theories.

Compare accounts and recognise opinion and possible bias

This follows on from the last point. You need to be aware that anything written by an individual is likely to be biased to some extent. In order to discern how biased a piece of writing is, you should be able to learn the purpose of a piece of writing and then compare it with other texts on similar subjects. In many cases, there is no single definitive account of a subject and so the more viewpoints you can compare, the better your understanding will be. A useful technique is to look for emotive phrases or images and ask yourself why they may have been used.

Synthesise the information you have obtained for a purpose

You need to take the information you have found and organise it in a way that demonstrates you have understood the main points, lines of argument and the differing viewpoints and accounts. You can then create a document or presentation that is unique to you and your understanding of the topic.

Writing

The final component of the Key Skills Communication portfolio revolves around the production of your own documents or texts.

As with reading, writing is an ancient skill that has been utilised in nearly all civilisations as a means of storing knowledge and ideas for future reference. Whilst the basics of writing are constant, ie writing words, there are a great many forms writing can take, eg letters, reports, novels, instructions, etc. All writing is designed to be read at some point and, therefore, successful writing will involve a consideration of who the writing is for (the audience) and its purpose.

Level 1

To achieve Level 1, you should be able to do the following.

Use different forms of presenting information

You should be aware that there are many ways to present written information and that you must produce **two different** texts, for example, letters, essays, reports, application forms, etc.

Use images to help the reader understand your main points

You should include either a picture, graph, table, or diagram in your document. These can help put across information that would otherwise take a long time to describe in words.

Judge the relevance of information and the amount to include for your purpose

You should remember the purpose of your document when you are deciding what to include. If your research has been successful, your task will involve deciding which points you can afford to leave out rather than trying to think of extra things to include. You should also decide on a balance between information and facts, and opinions and comments.

Make your meaning clear by writing, proofreading and redrafting documents so that:

- words you use most often in your work or studies are spelled correctly
- sentences are formed correctly
- sentences are marked by capital letters, full stops and question marks and organised into paragraphs where appropriate.

Clearly, you should take care when writing your documents. You can take several steps to ensure you reach the level of accuracy required.

Try to write your document in a single sitting away from distractions. This will allow you to concentrate on producing a coherent piece of writing and hopefully keep mistakes to a minimum.

Always try to check spellings you are unsure of, either by looking back at your research, using a dictionary or a word processor spellcheck.

Check through your writing when you have finished to see if any corrections are required. A good tip is to read it backwards as this stops you from skimming over mistakes without noticing them. Alternatively, you can ask someone else to read your work or use the spellcheck.

'The spell cheque has red yore work and found know errors'

Redrafting is a skill that many people fail to utilise. Redrafting should involve more than simply creating a neat copy of your document. You can make improvements to the structure, clarity and word choice when you redraft.

Level 2

To achieve Level 2, you should be able to do the following.

Present written information in different forms

You should try to include evidence of different forms of writing in your portfolio of evidence. You may have to practise writing formal letters, setting out questionnaires and assembling reports and essays.

Structure your material to help readers follow what you have written and understand the main points

It is important to recognise that the clarity of what you write can be enhanced by paying attention to the way you present your ideas as well as to the actual words you choose. This means that you should think in advance about what you want to include in your document and, in particular, about the order to present your ideas. Try to break up your content into clearly-defined sections. This will help you write at greater length and be more focused on each separate section. If you use clearly-separated paragraphs and then present them using headings and subheadings, other people will find it far easier to follow your arguments.

Use different styles of writing to suit different purposes

You should be clear about the purpose of your writing before you start. For example, if you are presenting factual material then you should keep your writing as clear and straightforward as possible so that someone else can follow exactly what you are trying to say. Alternatively, if you are trying to persuade someone to agree with a certain viewpoint then you may have to try and use a greater variation of sentence length and vocabulary in order to make your points stand out. For example, if you were trying to persuade someone that foxhunting was wrong then it might help to make the death of the fox sound particularly horrific. If you were trying to adopt the opposite view then you would try to make the damage caused by foxes sound especially bad.

Make meaning clear by writing, proofreading and redrafting documents so that:

- words most often used in your work or studies are spelled correctly and spelling of irregular words is checked
- complex sentences are formed correctly and organised into paragraphs where appropriate
- punctuation is accurate.

His notes clearly stated that he should proofread his wok...

You need to pay attention to the use of conjunctions (these are words that help join two sentences together). Common conjunctions include 'but', 'because', 'and', 'so' and 'then'. For example, look at the following two sentences:

The man fell off the wall.
He was pushed.

These sentences can be joined together to form a single complex sentence by using a number of different conjunctions:

The man fell off the wall **because** *he was pushed.*
The man fell off the wall **when** *he was pushed.*
The man fell off the wall **after** *he was pushed.*

You should also make sure that the tenses of your sentences are consistent. Think carefully about whether the things you are writing about have already happened, are happening now or are going to happen in the future.

For example, the following sentence does not make sense because its tenses are not consistent:

Yesterday, the dog was walking along and it is barking.

The first part of the sentence is taking place in the past. The second part of the sentence is taking place in the present. The sentence should read:

Yesterday, the dog was walking along and it was barking.

Level 3

To achieve Level 3, you should be able to do the following.

Select appropriate forms for presenting information to suit your purpose

In order to achieve Level 3, you need to produce two documents, one of which must be extended (at least three A4 pages long) on a complex subject. This means that it is very important for you to select the appropriate format to present your information. The most likely formats include extended essays and reports. Different forms are more appropriate for some tasks than others. For example, a piece of writing that considers different points of view and expresses your own opinions may be more suited to the flexible essay format. This could be the same for a task that requires you to explore ideas based on information that you have gathered. However, a piece of writing that explains the objectives, methods and results of an experiment, investigation or research will probably benefit from using the more rigidly-structured report format. These two formats are discussed in more detail below:

- **Extended essays** – Essay writing is likely to be a familiar task to many people taking the Key Skills qualification. However, as it is such an important medium for demonstrating knowledge, skills and understanding of a subject, it is worth spending some time considering how to write a successful essay.

  The word essay comes from the Old French *essai*, meaning 'to attempt'. An essay is likely therefore to be a response to a specific question that is seeking to elicit an **attempt** at an answer from you. This attempt should involve: thinking carefully about the question you are answering; gathering and collating relevant information; planning and sequencing your ideas; and, finally, writing your essay.

- **Reports** – Report writing requires you to use a more defined structure than essay writing (although both require thorough planning). A report is more likely to be arranged using clearly-headed sections. For example, hypothesis or aims, methods, results, findings, conclusions, etc. A report should also make greater use of graphs, diagrams and tables to help illustrate some of its information.

Select appropriate styles to suit the degree of formality required and the nature of the subject

It is important to remember that nearly everything you write is intended to communicate something to someone else. Thus, not only must your writing be as clear and organised as possible, but you must take the nature of the audience into account and adapt your writing accordingly, to fit their demands, capabilities and expectations.

Most writing that is undertaken in an academic context, ie in a school or college, will be of a fairly formal nature. Whether it is an extended essay or a report, there are conventions that should be adhered to. For example, there is a recognised way of incorporating quotations into English Literature essays. This involves setting the quotation in inverted commas to show that these words originate from a different source:

After killing Tybalt, Romeo declares that he is, "fortune's fool".

It is good practice to try and blend the quotation into your own sentence so that it still makes sense and flows smoothly.

When using longer quotations, it is better to separate the quotation from your own writing by leaving gaps at either end:

At the start of King Lear, *Lear announces,*

> *"Know that we have divided*
> *In three our kingdom; and 'tis our fast intent*
> *To shake all cares and business from our age,"*

This clearly introduces the catalyst for the action that is to follow.

Similarly, the tone or register of the language will be fairly formal with little use made of slang, colloquialisms or dialect. The reliance on Standard English in academic writing is probably based around a desire to make the language of learning equally accessible to all without discrimination.

The use of technical or specialist jargon should be carefully monitored and explanations or alternative terms provided, depending on the level of expertise of the intended audience.

The idea of considering the audience is also important if the subject of the writing is a potentially sensitive one, for example, racial issues.

The purpose of the writing also influences the style and tone of the language used. For example, a report requires a clear, factual tone that keeps opinions to a minimum and employs little in the way of figurative language.

If you are writing a persuasive or argumentative piece, you can draw upon a number of linguistic approaches:

- **Personal language** – By directly addressing an audience, you are more likely to establish a connection with them and make them agree with your point of view. For example:

  You *will undoubtedly have noticed how many opportunities are on offer here and* **you** *would be foolish not to take advantage of them.*

- **Emotive language** – By using words and phrases that appeal to people's emotions, you can draw their attention to what you are saying and begin to manipulate their responses.

His writing lacked emotive appeal

For example:

*The terrible **suffering** experienced by Native American Indians during the expansion of the settlers during the nineteenth century was widespread. **Starvation** and illness did not discriminate between the peaceful and the warlike, men and women or young and old, and nor did the greed of the white pioneers.*

The use of words like 'starvation' and 'suffering' immediately alert the reader to the writer's point of view and, because of the nature of the points they highlight, they make it harder to disagree with.

Organise material coherently

When you are creating extended documents on potentially complex subjects, you should plan out what you are going to include, leave out, and the sequence that you will present your ideas in before you begin to write.

If you are writing a report on an activity you have undertaken, you should begin by explaining what you have done and what you hoped to achieve. For example:

This report aims to examine the effects the construction of the new bypass has had on local trade in Newtown. It draws on information gathered from a survey of people's opinions and from information relating to previous bypass projects.

If you are writing an essay in response to a question, you should include an introduction that briefly sets out your answer to the question and how you intend to explain your answer. For example:

This essay aims to explore the question of whether Macbeth is a classic example of the tragic hero. It will consider the various definitions of the tragic hero and will consider the fate that Shakespeare creates for Macbeth in the play.

You should also plan the sequence of ideas in your writing. It is easier for a reader to follow your arguments or lines of thought if they are presented in a logical, connected order. For example, a report on the effectiveness of a company may include sections on the fabric of the building, the equipment, the salaries of the workforce, the past performance of the company, the recent record of the company, the performance of other companies who are in the same line of business, the profits, the future aspirations and plans, etc, etc. If you were writing this report, you would need to decide in which order to put the various sections. You should try to lead from one point to the next smoothly.

You may begin with a description and analysis of the most recent trading figures. This section might end with a phrase like the following:

...and so it can be seen that the last six months have seen a gradual rise in profits but at a slower rate than we **predicted**.

You then need to decide which section could follow on from this point most smoothly. The next section could open with:

These **predictions** *were based on our performance over the last three years...*

And conclude with:

...However, it should be remembered that we have invested heavily in our buildings and premises and this has temporarily restricted our short-term profits.

This, in turn, could lead to a discussion of the buildings, and so on, with each section neatly dovetailing with the next. The effect of this is to make it easy for a reader to understand the points you are attempting to communicate.

An additional technique that allows you to organise your writing is the use of textual navigational aids. These include headings and sub-headings, highlighting, indentation, underlining and the use of different fonts. These devices help to mark where sections of text start and finish and provide signposts for the reader. It is worth remembering that not all texts are designed to be read from start to finish. Consequently, anything that can help a reader locate a specific piece of information or reference quickly is useful.

'So... where do you want this signpost?'

Lastly, there are language features that can be employed to assist in the organisation and structuring of texts. Terms such as 'however', 'therefore', 'moreover' or 'furthermore' not only allow you to connect units of writing physically, but they also produce a conceptual linking of ideas. For example, 'therefore' allows you to connect a piece of evidence with a conclusion that can be drawn from it:

> *More trees in the rainforests were being chopped down each year;* **therefore***, animals were finding it harder to find food and shelter in their natural habitat.*

Words like 'furthermore' or 'moreover' allow you to expand upon ideas you are expressing in your writing. For example, a discussion of tourism levels could include:

> *The weather had been unusually good in Britain that year.* **Moreover***, a greater number of tourists had been able to use the new airport...*

'However' allows you to present exceptions or deviations from expectations or norms:

Manchester City had not played well for most of the season; **however,** *on the Saturday in question, their form took a turn for the better.*

Make meaning clear by writing, proofreading and redrafting documents so that spelling, punctuation and grammar are accurate

The importance of using Standard English in most academic writing has already been stressed. The need to make your writing as clear and easy to follow is essential, especially if qualifications depend on your being able to demonstrate knowledge and skills you have acquired to someone else, ie an examiner.

In order to achieve the necessary levels of clarity, it is important to check for possible errors and ways of improving your documents throughout all stages of the writing process.

Steps you can take to enhance the quality of your written work include:

- **Thorough planning** – If you have already considered the outline of your content, this will help the continuity and allow you to focus more on the actual process of writing.

- **Proofreading** – It is surprising how many errors can creep into a piece of writing despite numerous checks. It is always worth asking someone else to check your writing for you. Another proofreading strategy is to read the text from back to front as this prevents your eyes from skimming over what you have written and missing the opportunity to make corrections.

- **Making use of dictionaries and spellchecks** – Rules of grammar and spelling exist to make people's lives easier rather than harder. This is because the conventions of writing are there to ensure that what we write can be understood by others. Without rules, it is all too easy for meanings to be confused. Therefore, do not be afraid to make full use of any aid, either printed or electronic, that will help make your writing clearer.

- **Redrafting** – The most successful pieces of writing have usually been rewritten, altered and improved several times before they are considered finished. When writing an essay or a report, you should make a rough draft first. Then, read it through and think about how you could improve the expressions you have used, the clarity of your sentences and the order of your points. You should also consider redrafting as an opportunity to remove sections that do not seem as relevant or appropriate as they did when you started. At this stage, you can also introduce additional sections and expand upon existing parts of the document.

Wordsworth would soon reap the benefits of redrafting...

Part 2

Your portfolio

Your portfolio

You should now be aware that in order to gain the Key Skills Communication qualification, it is necessary to pass two distinct forms of assessment. One is the examination, which is dealt with in *Part 3* (see page 81). The other involves building up a portfolio or collection of evidence to demonstrate that you have mastered the necessary skills.

Collecting evidence

Evidence for your portfolio can take a variety of forms. For example, written evidence, graphs, maps, models or drawings, video footage, or recorded evidence from assessors, eg teachers. The last type of evidence is particularly relevant to Key Skills Communication, as it requires you to produce evidence of oral tasks such as discussions.

There was no way he was going to fail to gather evidence for his portfolio...

If you have designated Key Skills sessions then it is likely that you will undertake specific pieces of work or a course of study designed to allow you to demonstrate all the required Key Skills. It may be targeted at just the Communication element, or it may allow you to combine Communication skills with Application of Number and Information Technology.

Alternatively, you may be looking at the courses of study that you are following to find opportunities to demonstrate the Key Skills that this handbook discusses.

Whichever form your Key Skills supervision takes, you need to gather evidence of the skills you have mastered and record some details of the tasks you have completed. This is particularly relevant for the oral tasks of discussion and presentation. You can submit either audio or video evidence for these tasks, but you should keep a detailed written record as well.

Planning sheets

The planning sheets on the following pages can be used to record your achievements. In the space provided, describe how you have achieved each component of the Key Skills course. Each piece of evidence has been assigned a letter from **A** to **L** to help you identify them more easily. (These are used further in the sample assignment on pages 51 to 53.)

When you have completed a piece of evidence, remember to write the date and get your assessor (this could be your teacher) to initial the planning sheet.

Planning sheet: Discussion

You **must** contribute to a group discussion about a complex subject.

A Make clear and relevant contributions in a way that suits your purpose and situation.

Achieved	Date	Assessor

B Listen and respond sensitively to others, and develop points and ideas.

Achieved	Date	Assessor

C Create opportunities for others to contribute when appropriate.

Achieved	Date	Assessor

Please use the following space to record any additional information about your contribution to a discussion:

Planning sheet: Presentation

You **must** make a presentation about a complex subject, using at least one image to illustrate complex points.

D Speak clearly and adapt your style of presentation to suit your purpose, subject, audience and situation.

Achieved	Date	Assessor

E Structure what you say so that the sequence of information and ideas may be easily followed.

Achieved	Date	Assessor

F Use a range of techniques to engage the audience, including effective use of images.

Achieved	Date	Assessor

Please use the following space to record any additional information about your presentation:

Planning sheet: Reading

You **must** read and synthesise information from **two** extended documents about a complex subject. (One of these documents should include at least **one** image.)

G Select and read material that contains the information you need.

Achieved	Date	Assessor

H Identify accurately, and compare, the lines of reasoning and main points from texts and images.

Achieved	Date	Assessor

| | Synthesise the key information in a form that is relevant to your purpose. |

Achieved	Date	Assessor

Please use the following space to record any additional information about the texts that you have read (eg, a bibliography):

Planning sheet: Writing

You **must** write **two** different types of document about complex subjects. (One piece of writing should be an extended document and include at least **one** image.)

J Select and use a form and style of writing that is appropriate to your purpose and complex subject matter.

Achieved	Date	Assessor

K Organise relevant information clearly and coherently, using specialist vocabulary when appropriate.

Achieved	Date	Assessor

L Ensure your text is legible and your spelling, grammar and punctuation are accurate, so your meaning is clear.

Achieved	Date	Assessor

Please use the following space to record any additional information about your documents:

Gathering evidence
from assignments

You can produce a stand-alone project that enables you to
demonstrate your ability to cope with **all** the required skills.
The following pages offer an example of an assignment
and demonstrate how it covers all the elements of Key
Skills Communication.

The example given, which discusses issues relating to foxhunting,
is only a suggested proposal. Suitable topics include any other
debates or issues that are currently in the news. You could also
research the advantages and disadvantages of taking a gap year
after your post-16 studies or explore career opportunities resulting
from different academic subjects.

Sample assignment

Research the arguments surrounding the proposed law changes relating to the banning of foxhunting. You must gather information, write a report, present your findings to a group and then lead a discussion based on the ideas you have raised.

The following is a suggested list of stages you could go through to complete this assignment. Each circled letter, eg **D**, highlights which Key Skills Communication components are covered by each stage (these are described in full on the planning sheets on pages 42 to 49). It is extremely important that your own project covers each component from **A** to **L**.

Stage 1

Use a library, newspaper articles and the Internet to find information relating to foxhunting. This might include: contemporary opinions on hunting; the history of hunting; or scientific information relating to hunting, eg the effect of hunting on foxes or the damage they do. **G**

Write letters to organisations that may have information or strong opinions on the topic. You could also produce a questionnaire to gain information and opinion. These tasks would provide evidence of your non-extended written documents. **J** **K**

Stage 2

Look at the different opinions that individuals or groups of people have on the topic. Find out what evidence is given to back up these viewpoints. Look carefully at how this evidence is presented, including the use of pictures or statistical information. Remember to keep a note of the titles of the texts or Web sites you use. **H**

Stage 3

Make notes on your findings and keep them organised by using subheadings. This will make it easier to transform them into an extended piece of writing. Photocopy any images you wish to use as part of your writing or presentation. **Ⓘ**

Stage 4

Decide how you are going to structure your piece of writing. Separate out different aspects of the information you have found. For example, arguments for and against hunting. You could also include background material. It is important that you remember to include an image, perhaps a graph, table or photograph. Since this particular piece of writing is a report, keep the style of writing straightforward and formal.

Think carefully about the sequence of your paragraphs and the amount of specialist vocabulary you have used. **Ⓓ Ⓔ**

Stage 5

Once you have written your document, check it carefully for any corrections that are required to your spelling, grammar and punctuation. **Ⓛ**

Stage 6

It is now time to prepare the presentation. This can be closely based on your extended piece of writing, although you must remember that your information must now be listened to rather than read. Pay close attention to the order in which you present your ideas and, in particular, to the introduction which should clearly describe what you will be talking about. **Ⓓ Ⓔ**

Stage 7

Think carefully about how you present your ideas. Speak clearly and in a way that is appropriate for your audience. It is important that the audience can follow your lines of argument because they will need to discuss them. Utilise images, eg graphs or pictures, to help put across some of the complex ideas. **D F**

Stage 8

The final part of this assignment involves you leading a discussion with the audience of the presentation. It is important that you make several relevant contributions, perhaps clarifying points you made in your presentation or setting the agenda of the main points that should be discussed. However, it is equally important that you allow other people to develop their contributions so that the discussion can benefit from as many different viewpoints as possible. **A B C**

*'I have to admit, things **do** look different when viewed from here...'*

Gathering evidence from other subjects

If you are studying a range of subjects at AS/A-level or GNVQ, there are a number of opportunities for you to demonstrate the full range of skills required to gain your Key Skills Communication qualification.

You should discuss these opportunities with your teachers or supervisors, as they will be responsible for recording some of the evidence you require. This is particularly important when covering the discussion and presentation skills which need to be independently assessed.

It should be stressed that your teachers should not need to design special tasks in addition to your course requirements. One of the central ideas behind Key Skills is that you should be able to develop and perfect these skills as an inherent part of your day-to-day studies.

Every subject specification should contain information for teachers and students that directs them towards suggested examples of tasks and specific activities that allow you to demonstrate the Key Skills. You should also ask your teacher to show you examples from the Key Skills Support Programme subject files (see page 115). These show how Key Skills can be developed in AS/A-level subjects.

This section outlines recommendations for some of the subject areas. This will help you to manage your portfolio and, hopefully, build up all the evidence you need in the shortest possible time. The suggestions are based upon ideas given in the AS/A-level specifications from the AQA, Edexcel and OCR exam boards.

Art and Design

The study of Art and Design provides many good opportunities for accumulating evidence of Key Skills. These will be based around collaborative planning exercises, critical discussions and research tasks.

Discussion

Possible tasks include:

- Critical appraisal of your own and others' work – Evaluating the work of established artists or of people in your class.
- Consultation with staff and others – Discussing your own work at the planning stage, particularly with longer-term projects.

Presentation

Possible tasks include:

- Presentation to your peer group on art, design or craft issues – This may include evidence and examples of techniques and ideas from your own work that have either been successful or that have presented difficulties.
- Using slides, OHP, video or computer images – This could explore the work of a single artist, a movement or a critical issue, but the emphasis must be on the use of imagery.

Reading

You could research artists or movements, using different sources.

Writing

Possible tasks include producing:

- an annotated sketchbook that includes references to past and contemporary art and design, and a record of personal ideas.
- a piece of writing about an artist or movement that subsequently informs the development of your work.

Biology

Biology provides a range of opportunities for gathering evidence of Key Skills Communication. This is particularly true when planning or evaluating investigations or when responding to topical issues.

Discussion

AS/A-level Biology offers many opportunities for group discussion. The social and ethical implications of many topics are implicit and stated. A useful way of introducing ideas can be through newspaper or magazine articles on ethical issues which can then be developed.

Possible discussion topics include:

- The possible links between diet and coronary heart disease, supported by articles from the popular press, journals, CD-ROMs and the Internet.
- Contraception, *in vitro* fertilisation and abortion from biological and ethical viewpoints.
- The ethical implications of the use of AI (artificial intelligence), *in vitro* fertilisation and embryo transplantation in animals, and their social and ethical implications in humans.
- The advantages and disadvantages of genetic screening and the need for genetic counselling, supported by leaflets distributed by the Health Education Council.
- The effects and implications of ageing in the locomotory, nervous and sensory systems.

Presentation

Different components of the course could be presented using molecular building kits, computer-generated molecules from software (such as *Nemesis*), cut and paste shapes and photocopied resources.

Presentations could also be supported by electron micrographs and drawings on an overhead projector (prepared by hand or downloaded from a CD-ROM or the Internet) and by using prepared handouts.

Reading

Many opportunities for reading present themselves when preparing for discussion or presentation tasks. Use of the Internet, national newspapers and scientific journals will provide a fund of information to fulfil the evidence requirements.

Possible tasks include:

* Information from recommended textbooks and CD-ROMs plus data from a practical exercise could be used to illustrate the principles of enzyme action, and also to produce a coherent written account by hand or using a desktop publishing program.
* When studying human health and disease, use could be made of experimental evidence linking cigarette smoking and disease.

Writing

Most of the previously mentioned tasks and activities could be used as the basis of an extended written response, including revision notes and planning material.

Business Studies

Business Studies provides many opportunities to meet evidence requirements for Key Skills Communication, as successful business practice frequently involves confident and fluent communication.

Discussion

Possible discussion topics involve:

- The interaction between stakeholders and businesses, possibly involving examples from local businesses.
- The problems involved in measuring market share and market growth.
- The effectiveness of different motivation theories.

Presentation

You could make a presentation that follows on from any of the suggested discussion topics or you could base a presentation around your own research project.

Reading

You could research different motivation theories or organisation structures, either at a general theoretical level, or by looking at more specific examples of businesses. You could also use newspapers and magazines that deal with business issues as sources of relevant information.

Writing

Much of the assessment of any Business Studies course is dependent on written assignments. You should be able to use most essays, reports and projects, as well as some letters and formal communication with businesses, to meet the evidence requirements.

Chemistry

There are many opportunities within the course to produce Key Skills evidence based around the idea that Chemistry is subject to social, economic, environmental, technological, ethical and cultural influences.

Discussion

Many opportunities for discussion-based work arise during experimental group work. Other opportunities arise whilst studying the subject content of the course, particularly if considering social, economic or environmental issues.

Possible discussion topics include:

- Fuels – Pollution, new fuels, transport policy, etc.

- Halogenoalkanes – Environmental damage may result from the use of chemicals such as halogenated plastics and CFCs by society. Chemists may be involved with both the development of these chemicals and the search for alternatives and solutions to minimise any adverse effects.

- The contribution of chemistry to the quality of life and the economy of the UK. This could be set against the potentially damaging consequences of such activities for the environment and the role of chemists and national policy in minimising these.

Presentation

Most of the possible discussion topics could be extended to form the basis of a presentation to the rest of the group.

You could prepare a presentation based on posters which outline an environmental problem and the ways in which solutions can be provided by chemists, using relevant subject content.

This may include: developing new fuels, depletion of the ozone layer, the greenhouse effect, minimising car pollution, etc.

Reading

All the previously mentioned tasks and activities provide good opportunities for reading and synthesising information from a variety of sources.

Writing

Most activities on a Chemistry course require some form of written work, eg a standard laboratory write-up or a report from a full investigation.

Possible tasks include:

- Producing a document that traces the historical development of atomic structure or the Periodic Table.
- Producing a document on fuels, environmental issues, depletion of the ozone layer, the greenhouse effect, minimising car pollution, etc.
- When studying organic synthesis, producing a document that follows the development of a medicine.
- When studying spectroscopy, producing a document that summarises the theory behind modern spectroscopic methods.
- When studying the Periodic Table, producing a report on any aspect of elements or compounds using a range of resources (books, CD-ROMs, the Internet, etc).

Design and Technology

Design and Technology provides a rich source of evidence for Key Skills. Evidence can take the form of tutor observation records, preparatory notes, audio/video tapes, essays, etc.

Discussion

Possible discussion topics include:

- Market push and consumer pull.
- The influences of technological trends on the work of designers.
- How biotechnology has led to the development of new materials.

Presentation

Possible presentation topics include:

- The disassembly of products, using images and drawings to explain a product's construction.
- The impact of market trends on product specification.

Reading

Possible tasks include:

- Researching the use of ICT in manufacturing.
- Comparing and evaluating information about a range of products.
- Analysing research material to judge user needs.

Writing

Possible topics include:

- The buying behaviour and lifestyle of a target market group.
- The comparative testing of materials against specified standards.
- The impact of technical, economic, aesthetic, social, environmental and moral issues.

Economics

Economics is a subject that provides many opportunities for meeting the evidence requirements for Key Skills Communication. It is a subject that requires you to research, discuss and write about theories and models, and also investigate the practical applications and examples of those theories and models.

Discussion

Possible discussion topics include:

- The factors affecting public versus private versus merit goods, possibly using the National Health Service as a focus.
- The impact of environmental issues and government policy decisions affecting the UK economy.
- Advantages and disadvantages for the UK of monetary union within the European Union.
- The impact of national or international disputes on UK trade.

Presentation

You could make a presentation that develops ideas from the suggested discussion topics. It may be helpful to take roles during the discussion so that your group can explore a number of different viewpoints. Other presentation topics include:

- Evaluating different alternatives that objectives have, including profit maximisation.
- Outlining the spectrum of competition within market structure and examining these models in the light of firms' actual behaviour.

Reading

Possible topics include:

- The nature of markets and market structures.
- The impact of minimum wage legislation on the UK labour market.
- The impact of the government's policy on competition in tackling problems of market pressure.
- Research into the recent UK performance against other countries.

Writing

You will be able to meet the evidence requirements for writing through essays, projects and reports throughout the Economics course. Examples of the kind of tasks you might undertake include the following suggestions involving European issues:

- The nature of economic integration in a European context.
- Why competitive markets do not operate in EU agriculture.
- An analysis of living standards across Europe and the evaluation of policies to reduce these variations.
- The implications of European Monetary Union for its present and prospective members.

English

If you are studying either English Literature, English Language or English Language and Literature, you will be able to meet the evidence requirements for Key Skills Communication very easily. This is because this particular Key Skill is most closely connected to the skills that you will have learnt when studying English in the past.

Discussion

Discussions could be about a text that the group has read, either in terms of character or themes, or in terms of its composition and structure. Discussions could also be held on the group's own writing and problems they have encountered in attempting certain tasks, eg specific creative writing assignments.

Presentation

You could make a presentation about a text that you have read that serves as an introduction to a discussion of that text. You could also make a presentation about the development of a piece of your own writing. This may be a useful starting point for writing commentaries on your own creative writing assignments.

Reading

Clearly, English provides numerous opportunities to satisfy this particular element of the Key Skills Communication qualification. In addition to the texts you study, critical works and contemporary reviews will also allow you to meet the evidence requirements.

Writing

The English courses will all be assessed primarily through the writing of your own extended documents. It is important to remember that one of the pieces you use as evidence must contain an image.

General Studies

The broad sweep of topics and the frequent use of contemporary issues mean that you should easily be able to find a subject that allows you to develop the requirements for Key Skills Communication confidently.

Discussion

Any activities that involve group work or question and answer sessions (eg exploring opinions on topics raised by newspaper articles) should cover this element. Possible discussion topics include:

- The nature and value of formal education and whether schools should prepare students for the workplace.
- Ethics of genetic engineering – Benefits and drawbacks.
- Telecommunications – Availability, uses, benefits and drawbacks.

Presentation

Many opportunities exist for presentation following discussions or independent research.

Reading

Possible tasks include:

- Comparing editorials from different types of newspaper.
- Researching contributions in a particular field or area of interest.

Writing

Possible tasks include:

- An analysis of family breakdown and its impact on society.
- A newspaper report on waste disposal and recycling policies.
- A piece of writing that compares different sources of energy, eg the various benefits and drawbacks of nuclear power.

Geography

Geography draws on many different skills, ranging from discussions and debates to essay writing, to statistical analysis. Therefore, it is an ideal source of evidence for many of the Key Skills, including Communication.

Discussion

Many topics in Geography provide a suitable basis for a group discussion. The discussion must be about a complex subject and may be based on a number of ideas (some of which may be abstract, very detailed and/or sensitive). Specialist vocabulary may be used in the discussion. Opportunities that provide potential Key Skills evidence include:

- Coastal management strategies – Role-play/discussion of possible solutions, eg for Holderness.
- Rural change and conflict – Discussion of who owns the countryside in Britain, or options for change in a rural village.
- Flood protection strategies on river or coast – Role-play about possibilities, eg Towyn.
- Changing urban functions – Out of town versus Central Business District (CBD) debate.
- Environmental investigation – Discussion of fieldwork design and data collection.
- Threat to ecosystems – Group discussion of issues and solutions.
- Population control strategies – Discussion of means and solutions.
- Models of aid – Bottom-up/top-down, who is aid for?
- Group discussion – How can hazards be classified? What is wilderness?
- Issues analysis – Discussion/role-play as part of a local example.

Presentation

Key findings and conclusions resulting from coursework study could be presented to the rest of the group.

Possible tasks include:

- Multiple land uses in river catchment and/or multiple land uses at the coast – Production of conflict matrix and explanatory text. Wallchart with accompanying map of chosen catchment or coast.

- Sustainability in rural and urban areas – Read around ideas of sustainable rural areas/cities. Assess economic viability and feasibility of a range of schemes. Produce an article for a journal and a wallchart.

- Environmental investigation – Write-up and analysis. The finished report would be one full piece of evidence.

- Global warming research analysis – This could involve taking a topic raised in a contemporary news article and presenting it as the basis for further discussion.

Reading

Preliminary research for coursework should require you to read and synthesise information from a number of sources.

Extended documents may include textbooks, reports and articles of more than three pages. At least one of the documents must contain an image from which appropriate and relevant information can be drawn.

Possible areas of research include:

- Hard versus soft engineering – Use of two sources, eg an Environment Agency report, local council document, local newspaper article and technical journals. These will often have conflicting views.

- Hard versus soft engineering – Considering the issue of sustainability.

- Development strategies for rural areas in less economically developed countries (LEDCs) – Use of charity literature, government strategic plans, documents from agencies, eg the World Bank.

- Evaluation of urban regeneration strategies – International Institute for Environment and Development (IIED), etc, and articles in journals.

- Environmental investigation.

- Global warming – Research into opinions for and against issues relating to the human impact of global warming.

- Issues of international migration – Research into opinions on benefits and problems.

- Researching two types of document for assessment of chosen options.

Writing

All the potential topics for presentations could provide you with suitable assignments that will produce evidence for the writing element of Key Skills Communication.

History

History provides many opportunities for acquiring Key Skills Communication evidence because it is based around written texts, discussion and is also assessed through extended pieces of writing.

Discussion

Discussions about different kinds of sources and varied historical perspectives provide a range of opportunities. These could involve depth of study, change and continuity over an extended period, or a personal investigation. For example, 'The Development of Limited Monarchy in England, 1558-1689'. You are required to:

- understand a complex problem involving change and continuity over an extended period
- make relevant contributions about the extent of change
- respond to different views.

Presentation

Discussion topics can be adapted for presentations. You should structure ideas for the audience and use a range of techniques to relate to the audience's needs and feedback. Images might include pictorial material, tables or graphs, according to the nature of your investigation.

Reading

History presents a great many opportunities for reading that draws upon extended documents.

Writing

History offers a rich source of evidence for this element, since it is largely assessed through extended written answers.

ICT

ICT provides many opportunities for gathering Key Skills Communication evidence. This is particularly true when considering the practical applications of computers and connected technology. Practical applications of ICT which can help to improve your portfolio can be found on pages 79 and 80.

Discussion

Possible discussion topics include:

- The impact of ICT upon individuals, organisations and society.

- The effects of applications on society and the resulting need for retraining and reskilling humans to cope with changing work practices.

- The impact of external changes on an organisation, individuals within the organisation and on the systems in use.

You could also discuss how different factors have contributed to good design techniques for human–computer interfaces such as cognitive psychology, ergonomics, AI, design of computer input/output devices and software, including speech systems and visual systems.

Presentation

Possible presentation topics include:

- The social impact of ICT upon individuals – In terms of eroding work/social boundaries through teleworking; the ability to shop from home on the Internet; job satisfaction; ease of tasks; benefits to the disabled and elderly. Illustrations showing how teleworking can be implemented may be used.

- A presentation about how word processing and desktop publishing packages can be used with data from a spreadsheet or database for mailmerges and the benefits of this.
- A description of the ways in which numerical data can be presented graphically and how you can match appropriate types of chart to a given application, task or area.
- The facilities available on modern telephone systems and ISDN, and their limitations for handling data traffic.

Reading

In the definition, analysis and design section of the project, you are required to explain the user's requirements and how they were obtained. You need to synthesise the key material in order to evaluate alternative approaches to solve the problem.

Writing

You could describe a wide range of health and safety issues related to working with ICT, and suggest appropriate measures for avoiding health problems.

You are expected to use different forms and styles of writing in your design specification (this may include the method of solving a problem, such as the use of data structures) and documentation (for example, user documentation including images of the interface to the system).

Mathematics

Mathematics may not seem to provide evidence of Key Skills Communication quite as readily as more language-based areas of study. However, there are still several potential ways of building up your portfolio from this subject.

Discussion

You could use a mechanics kit to explore friction when studying the equilibrium of a particle. This work could be organised to produce evidence from discussions between groups.

If you are studying representation of data or bivariate data and collect your own data as part of the learning process, you could discuss details of the methodology and any problems you encounter.

If you have completed a research project, you could present your findings to a group and then take part in a question and answer session.

Presentation

Possible tasks include:

- Carrying out experimental work to investigate the modelling of friction when studying materials and presenting the conclusions to the rest of the group.

- Analysing a set of raw data and presenting your conclusions to the rest of the group.

- Presenting findings from a research project to the rest of the group.

Reading

If you submit a maths project, you will be able to draw on this for evidence. All candidates will practise the skill of extracting relevant information from various sources to provide data for calculations. Such sources could be in a variety of forms, including tables, charts, diagrams and graphs, and could include redundant information, requiring a selection to be made.

You should be able to extract important features from a table or statistical diagram and summarise your conclusions in words.

Whatever the nature of your project, you should use reference material, and extract and organise information in preparing the write-up.

Writing

You should be able to use mathematical expressions, graphs, sketches and diagrams with accuracy and skill, and to use mathematical language correctly to proceed logically through extended arguments. These skills enable you to demonstrate evidence of an appropriate form of written presentation and use of specialist vocabulary.

In studying numerical methods for the solution of equations, you could compare different methods for a variety of equations, including cases where a method failed, and then present the findings as an extended document.

A number of mechanics topics, eg using a mechanics kit, might lead to a written report in which conclusions are presented and which contain appropriate images and diagrams. Possible topics include friction, centre of mass and moments, and elasticity.

Data collected or analysed might form the basis of a written report which would include relevant graphs and diagrams.

Modern Foreign Languages

As a language-based subject, the study of Modern Foreign Languages provides many opportunities for gathering evidence of the Communication Key Skill. However, you should remember that, although a foreign language can be used to practise and develop the Key Skill, evidence must only be provided in English.

Discussion

Most of the AS/A-level specifications require you to discuss a variety of topics connected with the society and culture of the language or country you are studying.

Presentation

Any study of a different country requires information to be drawn from a wide variety of fields. This is likely to be useful if you research a number of these topics, eg food and tourism, and present them to the rest of your group or class.

Reading

Obvious opportunities for reading also exist in preparing the above presentations. Information can be found from a wide range of textbooks and Web sites.

Writing

There are many opportunities for writing essays or reports based on literature, culture and society.

Music

Music provides a number of opportunities for providing evidence of Key Skills Communication. It is a subject that requires you to discuss and present your ideas to others, and also to investigate the historical background and wider implications of the subject area.

Discussion

Possible topics for discussion include:

- How composers interpret extra-musical ideas.
- The creative tension between music and drama.
- The relationship between music and its wider context.

Presentation

You could prepare a presentation on the construction, sound properties and characteristics of your instrument in the context of learning about the expressive use of instrumental techniques. You may also find it useful to give presentations to your group before you prepare a written piece of work.

Reading

You will need to demonstrate knowledge and understanding of appropriate historical background. Possible topics include:

- The language of Western tonal harmony.
- The development of instruments and instrumental combinations.
- Working practices and performing conditions.
- Styles and techniques of composition.

Writing

Most of the above discussion and research topics could be used as a basis of an extended written response.

Physics

Physics provides a range of opportunities for gathering evidence for Key Skills Communication. This is particularly true when planning or evaluating investigations or when responding to topical issues involving practical applications of Physics.

Discussion

Many opportunities exist throughout the course for group discussion about complex subjects. Sources for the generation of such subjects include television programmes, newspaper articles, papers in scientific journals on topical research, or simply in the development of concepts in a practical lesson.

A possible topic is a discussion of the safety features in cars. The focus of the discussion might be on how the properties required of seat belts, air bags and crumple zones affect the design of such safety features.

Presentation

There are a number of opportunities which allow you to prepare and deliver a presentation that covers one or more of the evidence requirements. This might involve performing and explaining a demonstration experiment that would normally have been carried out by the teacher.

For a theoretical topic, material may be gained from secondary sources such a reference library or the Internet. You could vary the presentation technique by considering:

- the use of models to simulate the teaching point
- using ICT to produce static or video images
- the involvement of the audience through questioning or by other means.

A possible task could involve: studying the nuclear atom; researching α particle scattering equipment and the evidence it provides for the existence of charge and the small size of the nucleus; and then delivering a presentation of the findings. Alternatively, you could demonstrate electron diffraction to a class and explain the significance of the effect with respect to the spacing of atoms.

Reading

You should be reading sources that go beyond your course texts, for example, *New Scientist*, *Physics Review*, current newspaper articles, etc. You should extract relevant information and acknowledge lines of reasoning. It might be appropriate as part of your preparatory work for a topic to direct your background reading, for example, to the history of the discovery of radioactivity.

A possible task might involve reading about the handling, storage and disposal of radioactive materials. Alternatively, you could research circumstances in which resonance is useful and other circumstances in which resonance should be avoided.

Writing

Throughout the course, you will be writing up pieces of practical work or research. You should select at least one task that includes numerical data, allowing you to organise the information clearly in the form of tables and graphs.

A possible task might include determining the Young modulus of a metal when studying electrons and protons. You could write up a report of your experiment, tabulating the data, producing an appropriate graph and, subsequently, making conclusions.

Alternatively, you could take appropriate measurements to enable you to sketch the current-voltage characteristics of a filament lamp and then write up a report using your knowledge of Physics to explain the shape of the graph obtained.

Religious Education

Religious Education provides many opportunities for gathering Key Skills Communication evidence, particularly in areas where topics with many different ethical and moral viewpoints are being discussed. Much of the assessment is carried out through extended written tasks.

Discussion

Possible discussion topics include:

- The classical versions of arguments for the existence of God.
- The various views on the validity of the ethical basis of the Just War theory.

Presentation

Possible topics include:

- The geographical and religious context of pre-Islamic Arabia that shows trade routes and surrounding populations.
- The demographic distribution of Jews before and after the Holocaust.

Reading

Possible tasks include:

- Different views on the application of ethical theory to questions of euthanasia, both religious and non-religious.
- Comparing the main characteristics of several Hindu deities, including their traditional representations in images.

Writing

You should be able to develop nearly all the suggested topics for discussion, presentation and reading to produce suitable pieces of written work to meet this element of Key Skills Communication.

Using ICT

Information and
Communication
Technology can be
used in a variety of
ways to improve and
extend your portfolio.
It is worth exploring
the various packages
and technologies that
you may have access to,
as well as asking for
help with areas of ICT
about which you
are unsure. Suggestions
as to how you could use different software packages and the
Internet are given below.

Word processing/desktop publishing

Using a word processor or desktop publishing program to produce
material in your portfolio (eg reports and extended essays) means
that you can produce legible written documents more easily than
if they are handwritten. The drafting process can be simplified by
manipulating text using the cut, copy and paste facilities. Accuracy
can be improved by using grammar and spellcheckers. You can
also use a range of presentational features such as different fonts,
colours and heading sizes. Not only do these make the work
appear more attractive, but they can help readers to navigate the
text, making it easier to understand.

Spreadsheets

Spreadsheets are very versatile and can be useful when analysing and presenting material in your portfolio. They can be used to produce graphs and charts and also to perform calculations. Spreadsheets can be included in written documents, but are also very effective when used as prompts and handouts for presentations and discussions.

Databases

A database is a program that stores data. It can be used to search and sort data and to print out reports. This is a very useful function if you wish to analyse raw data, eg from a questionnaire.

Presentations

If you are able to use a presentation package (eg Microsoft® PowerPoint) then you will instantly be able to make more of an impact in the discussion and presentation elements of Key Skills Communication. The combination of clearly-presented information, together with moving images and sound, can help you focus your audience's attention on specific elements of your talk. However, you still need to work carefully on the preparation of your presentation, as the graphics will only be of use if your ideas have substance.

The Internet

If you have access to the Internet then you should be able to find plenty of relevant material to help you prepare for discussions and presentations. However, if you use the Internet, it is important to be selective as not all material will be relevant. You will not gain any marks for simply printing off documents that have a relevant title.

Part 3

The examination

The examination

In addition to assembling your portfolio of evidence, you must also pass an externally-verified examination called an External Assessment Instrument (EAI) in order to achieve your Key Skills Communication qualification. The examination can be taken at a number of times throughout the year (examinations are usually held in November, January, May, June, August and September) and can be retaken if you do not pass at the first attempt. The examination lasts for 90 minutes and takes the form of a reading comprehension. You will usually have to read three documents and answer a series of questions on them that are worth a total of 50 marks. The questions are divided into two sections:

- Short answer questions (worth 25 marks)
- Long answer section (worth 25 marks).

'Your assignment, should you choose to accept it...'

Short answer questions

You will need to answer approximately five questions (sometimes more or less) that require you to:

- **select** and **read** material that contains information you require
- **identify accurately** and **compare** the lines of reasoning and the main points from the documents
- **synthesise** the key information in a form that is relevant to a given purpose.

Exam tips

Read each question carefully so you are clear about exactly what you are being required to do. There is no point in wasting valuable time commenting at length on something if you are simply being asked to select and list specific information.

Students often drop pints by misreading the question!

Similarly, if you are asked to synthesise material (reproduce it in a different form), you will lose marks if you fail to put it into your own words.

Try to establish **who has written the text** and what point of view they might hold. This will help you to understand the context of the material and also any possible lines of reasoning. For example, it may be significant that text comes from either a tabloid or a broadsheet newspaper. Alternatively, it could be attributed to an individual or be written on behalf of an organisation.

Try to establish the **purpose** of the text. This will also help you to identify and follow lines of reasoning. For example, a text may be trying to present a balanced argument that takes more than one point of view into account. Alternatively, it could be attempting to persuade readers to agree with one particular point of view. It is important to be aware of potentially biased writing.

Try to establish the **intended audience** for the text. For example, a text may be targeted primarily at people who the writer assumes already agree with him or her, eg an article in support of gun ownership in a shooting magazine. Alternatively, the text may be aimed at a particular gender, social class, level of education, etc.

It is a good idea to **read through the questions quickly** before you read the texts so that you know what information you are looking for and can then read strategically.

As you read the texts, do not hesitate to **make notes and highlight or underline relevant material** as you find it. Using coloured pens or pencils to identify material that is relevant to different questions can also be useful.

It is best to **read a whole text through** to the end before starting to write an answer. This will enable you to gain a more coherent understanding of the points and arguments that are being presented.

You need to **judge how long to spend on each question** in the short answer section (this usually accounts for 45 minutes or half the total time of the exam). The best way to do this is to check how many marks each question is worth. If they are worth roughly equal marks then dividing up your time

Some questions were harder than others...

is a relatively straightforward task. However, you do need to be careful because one question (sometimes the last one) is sometimes worth more marks than the others. This means you have to ensure that you leave sufficient time to gain all the marks that are available.

If you need to check back through the texts, it is useful to be able to **scan or skim the material** rather than reading it all from top to bottom. In order to do this, note down the sequence of ideas and points next to the text. For example, the first three paragraphs may contain background information, the middle paragraphs may outline a problem, and the final paragraphs may offer suggested solutions to that problem. Having done this it will be easier to locate information relating to one of these particular sections in order to answer a later question.

Additionally, you should try to **utilise any headings or subheadings or the first paragraphs of separate sections** of a text as these will help you navigate swiftly around a text and locate information you may need.

Long answer section

In this section you need to provide one extended answer to a question that requires you to:

- use a format and style of writing that is appropriate to the purpose
- organise the relevant material from all the named documents clearly and coherently
- use your own words and specialist vocabulary where appropriate
- write legibly using accurate spelling, punctuation and grammar.

Exam tips

Read the question very carefully to establish exactly what you are being asked to do. You need to judge the audience and purpose of your writing in order to select an appropriate format and style, eg a formal letter, report, etc.

Plan your writing carefully – You will be required to draw on information from all the documents you have read. It is especially important to spend some time carefully selecting the information that is relevant and considering the sequence in which you will present your ideas.

Concentrate on **linking pieces of information** from the source documents coherently, using quotations and citing references where appropriate.

Concentrate on **presenting your work neatly**. Do not rush – it is more important to aim for quality than quantity.

Leave some time at the end of the examination to check back through what you have written so that you can amend any errors and make any improvements that you think are necessary. It is always better to spend the last minutes of any examination ensuring that what you have written is correct rather than adding one or two extra points. The examiner will already have a good impression of your level of ability and you are very unlikely to change their opinion within the space of a couple of extra lines.

Worked examination

The following pages show you the format of a past Key Skills Communication exam (from November 2000). Sample answers and explanations of how marks are awarded are provided on pages 100 to 103.

This exam is constructed around three texts taken from three different newspapers: the *Guardian*, *Express* and *London Evening Standard*. Each text provides different information relating to London's Millennium Dome (now no longer open).

Space for notes is provided next to the source documents.

Millennium Dome

Document 1

"I paid up, I queued up, and now I'm thoroughly fed up. As one of its early supporters, I'm sorry to say that the Dome is a lemon," says Polly Toynbee.

This is not an I-told-you-so column. Quite the contrary, I didn't. I was not among the multitude who wished the Dome ill, hoped it wouldn't open in time or complained of its monumental cost.

But, alas, this is not a great exhibition. It is a deep disappointment. It does not work on any level, from the most mundane purchase of a cup of coffee to any bit of really good fun.

As a Dome enthusiast, I bought ten tickets ages ago to take my family for the day: £20 a head didn't seem exorbitant for the 'Amazing Day' promised. All that was required was a bit of Wow! Any old Wow! would have done – fantastic rides, an amazing spectacle, something witty, startling futurism, geewhiz science, anything memorable would do.

The trouble with queuing is that expectations rise exponentially with every minute queued. If you stand outside the body zone for an hour, it had better be worth it, but all you get is seven minutes

of nothing much. The mildly surreal
beating of a heart or Tommy Cooper's
brain telling jokes is an utterly inadequate
reward for those who have queued angrily
for so long.

And there were queues for almost
everything worth seeing (none for the faith
zone), so in eight hours I couldn't see all
the zones. Maybe I missed something
wonderful but I doubt it. Who are we, one
zone asks? British patience suggests we are
people who queue with pride, the same
old British psyche that celebrates the
Dunkirk spirit. There was no rebellion,
have-a-nice-day hosts were not lynched
and no one ran amok, although we
queued 45 minutes for coffee and after
queuing for an hour in what looked like
the shortest food queue, we were
eventually told that the food had run out.

But the serious problem was that
there was nothing worth queuing for.
At a breezy gallop the whole
experience could be quite fun.
But in the play zone, with long queues
for each item, none of the games
approach the ones the kids have
at home. Parents of young children
were complaining bitterly at how
bored they were. Teenagers made
disparaging comparisons with modern
arcade machines.

Everywhere high-minded messages are
matched with low-tech exhibits. Nothing

here is as astounding as the Internet,
nothing is as creative as the best television
programmes, all of it assembled by
exhibition organisers with nothing to
exhibit. The best space is wasted on a vast
auditorium for a show of ugly banality:
the West End does better with any
musical. The Dome can't contend with
state-of-the-art modern entertainment.

If they had acknowledged that problem
from the start, they would have handed
the central theme over to artists, the only
begetters of anything good here. What's
memorable is the building itself, grubby
by day but startling when lit at night, like
an iridescent jellyfish. But there never
could have been message or meaning in an
exhibition of this kind. The lesson is that
only those elements created by artists have
meaning. Sadly, they are too few and far
between to rescue the Dome, but in future
this should tell governments to rely on
artists whose work will outlast them.

*(Adapted from an article in the
Guardian, 5 January 2001)*

Document 2

"Celebrate this great British achievement." As the Dome comes in for criticism, Peter Mandelson gives it the thumbs-up.

When I stopped being Dome Minister a year ago, I gave a parting warning to the excellent team working on the project, "If you think things have been hard going so far, wait until the Dome opens," I told them. "Because that's when the carping will really start."

After its first week up and running, we should not care about what some of the press are saying about the Dome. As any politician, any entertainer, anyone in the public eye knows, there is only one thing that counts – what the public thinks. And the reaction from people paying their money is overwhelmingly positive: they are leaving Greenwich after one amazing day out, with smiles on their faces. And better than that, they are saying that they will recommend the Dome to their friends.

It is not the critics who ensure success, it is the paying public – and their first reactions make me confident that the Dome is going to be a success. Staff are recording high levels of satisfaction and enthusiasm. Visitors are telling them that they didn't believe what some of the press was saying – and now they know for a fact that the negative stories just aren't true. Nobody is claiming that everything is perfect. But, as any good business would do, staff are listening to visitors to make a day at the Dome even better.

Visitors explore the world in which we live together, play together and, yes, even occasionally queue together. There are queues for the most spectacular bits of the Dome but I would be rather worried if there were not, especially when the schools are on holiday. There's many a cinema or theatre manager who would pray for a queue at the box office. But the Dome is working to keep those queues moving and to make sure that people know how long they have to wait. The average queue is five minutes – that's not to say that there aren't some that are longer, but everyone is learning to manage the flow of visitors to increase people's enjoyment.

There has never been a time in the history of these islands when we have had so many leading lights in so many fields of creativity: film, fashion, architecture and art. The Dome is, quite simply, a celebration of this creativity and inspiration, and is being recognised as such internationally. If readers of some of our newspapers could see how the international media have reported the Dome, they would get an entirely different perspective and a story that is inspirational, not derogatory.

It will assuredly bring big rewards on top of the fun and excitement for families from all over the country. Foreign visitors to the Dome will contribute an additional £1 billion to the British economy this year. About 13 000 people have gained work in the construction and operation of the Millennium Experience. Greenwich Council tells me that it estimates that over the next seven years, a further 25 000 jobs will be created locally as a result of the Dome's regenerative impact on one of the poorest areas of the capital and country. That, I think, is quite an achievement – one to be proud of, not to criticise.

I am proud that we are the only country to have created a year-long attraction to celebrate the new millennium, rather than a five-minute wonder on New Year's Eve. And we have done so without a single penny of tax-payers' money.

The creators of the Dome set out to achieve a mixture of "fun and education under one roof". Please don't just take my word for it. Go and see for yourself. Treat yourself and enjoy One Amazing Day.

(Adapted from an article in the Express, *9 January 2001)*

Document 3

Dome welcomes results of first independent poll – Published in the *London Evening Standard*

505 visitors to the Dome were asked for their views on their day at the Dome.

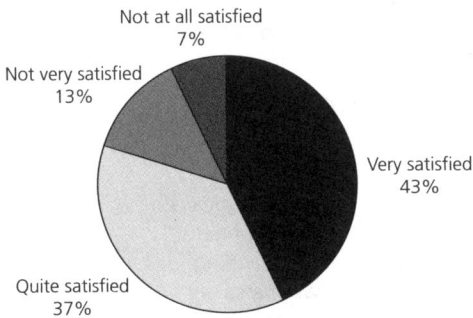

A massive 71% said that they would recommend the Dome to their friends!

This chart shows where the visitors to the Dome came from on that day:

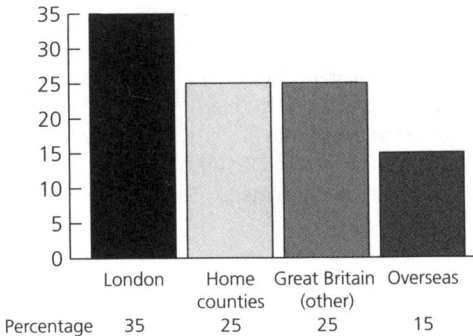

	London	Home counties	Great Britain (other)	Overseas
Percentage	35	25	25	15

Short answer questions

NB Always take note of which source documents each question is asking you to consider.

1 Using information from Document 1, answer the following questions.

Polly Toynbee criticises the contents and the organisation of the Dome. Select (a) **two** pieces of evidence she gives to support her criticisms of the contents and (b) **two** supporting her criticisms of the organisation. *(4 marks)*

Hints: The keyword in this question is select. This means that you only have to find the required information and write it down. It is not necessary to spend time adding any of your own comments or opinions. Two marks are available for part (a) and two marks for part (b), so make sure you differentiate between content and organisation.

2 For this question use Document 2. In his defence of the Dome, Peter Mandelson puts forward a series of arguments. Using your own words, briefly outline **four** of these arguments. *(5 marks)*

Hints: This question requires you to read the text carefully and identify four lines of reasoning from the document. Each argument you identify is worth one mark. One mark is also available for taking the information and writing it in your own words. Do not be tempted to simply copy or quote the main points.

3 Use Documents 1 and 2 for this question. The
   two writers make contradictory statements
   about the queues inside the Dome. Identify
   two such statements from each document
   and compare the different reasoning that
   the writers use.   *(5 marks)*

   Hints: This question asks you to consider two of the
   documents and compare the lines of reasoning used in
   each. Two marks are awarded for identifying two
   statements from each passage. The fifth mark is awarded
   for presenting your comparison in a clear and
   appropriate form.

4 Do the accompanying charts (Document 3)
   best support Toynbee's or Mandelson's arguments?
   Compare the evidence from the charts with
   the writers' arguments and give reasons to
   support your answer.   *(5 marks)*

   Hints: This question requires you to select information
   from pictorial sources. It is important when using graphs
   and tables to check carefully what they are illustrating.
   You can do this by reading the headings and labels
   carefully and by ensuring you have checked the scales
   they are using. For example, a graph could be showing
   actual numbers of people who have visited the Dome or
   it could be showing percentages. One mark in this
   question is available for selecting the relevant
   information, two further marks are for comparing it with
   the writers' arguments, and a further two marks are
   available for presenting your findings in a way that
   demonstrates that you have followed the writers' lines
   of reasoning.

5 Use Documents 1 and 2 for this question. The writers express different views about the contribution made by artists and other creative people in the design of the Dome exhibition. Compare their lines of reasoning and identify **two** key points made by each author to support their case. *(6 marks)*

Hints: You should consider the ideas expressed in both texts carefully and select the relevant information, even though it may be contradictory. This task is worth five marks but you need to find two points made by each writer. The final mark is again awarded for expressing your answer clearly.

Extended answer question

Question 6

You have received a request (in English) from the mayor of a European town twinned with your own. She is considering organising a trip to the Dome and would value information and comments from you in the light of the controversy she has read about in the press. Write a formal letter to the mayor, making sure that you include both sides of the argument (as expressed in the documents provided) and giving your own opinion.

The address for the letter is:

The Mayor
Anytown
Anywhere
Europe
EU53469   *(25 marks)*

Hints

The extended task allows, by its very nature, for a wider variety of possible answers than the short answer section. However, in these types of tasks marks are always awarded for certain identifiable achievements.

In the case of this example, you will be awarded marks for:

Structure:

Presenting the information in an appropriate form, eg a formal letter. This will mean setting out the letter correctly, adopting an appropriate syntax (sentence structure), tone and vocabulary. *(5 marks)*

Content:

- Organising the information clearly in linked paragraphs. *(2 marks)*
- Presenting the arguments clearly and cogently. (This carries the most marks as it is liable to vary the most between different candidates and levels of ability.) *(6 marks)*
- Presenting a sensible personal opinion based on the evidence from the articles. *(2 marks)*

Accuracy and legibility:

- Legible writing. *(1 mark)*
- Between one and nine marks are available for accuracy. *(9 marks)*
  These are awarded as follows:
  - Up to three marks are available for a candidate who spells, punctuates and uses the rules of grammar with **reasonable** accuracy; and uses a **limited range** of specialist terms appropriately.
  - Up to nine marks are available for a candidate who spells, punctuates and uses the rules of grammar with almost **faultless** accuracy; and uses a **wide range** of specialist terms adeptly and with precision.

Sample answers

These answers are intended to demonstrate both an appropriate style and a suitable level of detail for answering these types of examination questions. Therefore, they do not include every point that could be relevant for each question, but simply the correct number to earn the available marks. For example, if two marks are available for two points then that is all that has been included.

Question 1

a   Polly Toynbee criticises the contents of the Dome. In order to back up her claim, she suggests that, in the play zone, the available games are not even as good as the ones the kids have access to at home. She also points out that the contents of the body zone are an 'utterly inadequate reward' for the time spent in the queues to gain entry to it.

b   She also criticises the organisation of the Dome and, in particular, the length of the queues. She mentions that so much time was spent waiting that it was impossible to see all the exhibits in eight hours. A further piece of evidence she cites is that the available food ran out.

Question 2

Peter Mandelson presents several arguments in defence of the Dome. He says that the staff at the Dome have been listening to the public and are reporting high levels of approval. He also claims that any negative reporting from the press is far less important than what the public say.

He goes on to focus on the economic impact of the Dome by pointing out that not only has it directly provided 13 000 jobs but it will also continue to have a positive impact on the surrounding area. Mandelson also points out that the Dome acts as a celebration of British creativity and artistic talent.

Question 3

Both writers discuss the queues but draw very different conclusions. Polly Toynbee writes that she had to wait an hour in order to gain entry to the body zone and 45 minutes just to buy a cup of coffee. She argues that the longer the time spent waiting, the greater the expectation and, consequently, the greater the disappointment when you are finally able to see exhibits (that she was clearly not impressed by).

Peter Mandelson approaches the subject of queues from a different angle. He emphasises how well the queues, which he considers to be worthwhile as they are for the most 'spectacular' parts of the Dome, are managed. He points out that the staff are continually learning how to improve the flow of people and that the public are constantly kept informed about how long they will have to wait.

Question 4

The evidence in Document 3 backs up the arguments of Peter Mandelson. The pie chart clearly shows that 80% of the visitors in the survey were at least quite satisfied and, of them, 43% stated they were very satisfied. The statistics also claim that 71% of visitors would recommend the Dome to their friends. This evidence supports Mandelson's claims that public reaction to the Dome was positive. The graph also demonstrates that 15% of visitors are from overseas which goes some way to supporting his claim that the Dome has a good reputation in other countries.

Question 5

The two writers express different views about the contribution made to the Dome by artistic and creative people. Polly Toynbee bemoans the fact that creative people seem to have had very little input into the Dome. She criticises the central show for being ugly and banal and failing to compare with West End musicals. She goes on to suggest that only the exhibits created by artists have meaning and there are not enough of these to make the exhibition worthwhile.

Peter Mandelson agrees that Britain does have a great many talented, artistic people, but he suggests that the Dome is a celebration of this talent. He feels this is confirmed by the way the foreign press acknowledges what has been achieved in the Dome.

Question 6

The Mayor
Anytown
Anywhere
Europe EU53469

8th May 2000

Dear Madam

Thank you so much for your recent enquiry about the Millennium Dome. I fully appreciate that you may have reservations about going ahead and organising a trip to this attraction and I am only too happy to provide you with some extra information that may help you reach a satisfactory decision on this matter.

The sheer scale of the Millennium Dome project seems to have raised people's expectations of it, along with many other aspects of the Millennium, to unrealistic heights. It is, therefore, hardly surprising that many of the reactions to the Dome that you will have read in the press have been critical and indeed, disappointed. Some commentators have dismissed the Dome by saying it lacks a 'wow' factor. This may be due to the build up of excitement that people are experiencing as they queue to see the most popular zones. It could therefore be a consequence of the exhibits' failure to match people's heightened expectations rather than to any inherent failings they may have. It should also be pointed out that according to surveys of the visitors, the vast majority of people claim to have enjoyed their visit to the Dome.

The queues at the Dome have become an important issue. Queues are arguably an unavoidable feature of an attraction that has successfully generated great public interest. There have been reports of people waiting for up to an hour for certain exhibits and for 45 minutes to buy a cup of coffee. It is unclear how representative these experiences are, but the ex-Dome Minister, Peter Mandelson has commented that the average queuing time is only five minutes and that the public are kept fully informed of how long they may have to wait. Most importantly, the staff are constantly seeking to improve the flow of visitors around the Dome. I will leave you to decide if this situation is unreasonable or not but it does seem as if steps are being taken to improve things all the time and so the situation may be more reliable in the future should you decide to go ahead with your visit.

The contents of the Dome have also been the subject of debate. Critics have suggested that the exhibits compare unfavourably with other modern sources of entertainment such as: computer games, television or West End shows. However, defenders of the Dome's reputation have argued that it does provide a wide variety of high quality entertainment that represents some of the best creative thinking in Britain.

Lastly, I feel that it should be stressed that 71% of visitors to the Dome have claimed that they would recommend the experience to their friends. It should also be pointed out that 15% of the Dome's total visitors are from overseas and so it must be concluded that the majority of people who have made the effort to journey to Britain in order to experience the Millennium Dome have come away feeling the trip was worthwhile.

I do hope that I have gone some way to removing some of your reservations concerning a visit to the Millennium Dome and that you will be organising your trip in the not too distant future. If there are any points on which you require further information, please do not hesitate to contact me.

Yours faithfully

Nick Kiernan

Practice examination

Document 1:
Pros and cons of GM foods

Notes

Genetic modification means copying and transplanting a gene from one organism to another and altering ('modifying') it in a way that cannot come about naturally, for instance, by inserting a gene from an arctic flounder into a plant's genetic code (DNA) to make it frost-resistant. Biotechnology companies use genetic modification to improve a crop's resistance to weeds, to increase yields or speed up growth cycles.

There's intense debate over genetic modification. Some people believe it is tampering with nature and 'playing God'. Another belief is that patenting GM processes will lead to increased commercialisation of nature as companies own the rights to GM patents.

However, GM crops that are pest resistant and give higher yields could provide enough food for the growing world population.

In addition, plants could be modified to produce more nutritious or healthier foods and could be developed to survive in extreme conditions like droughts.

Pesticides and herbicides may be used less intensively with energy savings from reduced crop spraying.

GM food could have health benefits, such as providing edible vaccines, as well as providing cheaper, better quality and tastier food.

On the other hand, we do not know enough about what will happen to genes inserted into GM crops.

Growing GM crops on a large scale may have implications for biodiversity, the balance of nature, wildlife and the environment.

Genes from GM crops could transfer to non-GM crops and other plants growing nearby.

Animals could be exploited. Research is looking at ways to make animals grow faster and supply organs for human transplantation.

(Adapted from Which?, *March 1999)*

Document 2: Gene cuisine

Reading the labels on food won't necessarily tell you if the ingredients have been genetically modified.

Concern about genetically-modified food is widespread, yet many of us may be eating food containing GM ingredients without realising it. This is despite European labelling regulations, introduced in September 1998, to help consumers identify GM ingredients in their foods, because manufacturers aren't always required to do so by the regulations.

GM soya and maize

GM soya and maize are now approved as safe for use in Europe. Soya is currently one of the main sources of genetically-modified ingredients in food. It is estimated that 40% of last year's US soya crop was genetically modified. Brazil and Argentina, the other main exporters of soya beans, are now growing GM varieties, too.

Most of our soya is imported from the US and contains a mixture of GM and non-GM soya beans. Suppliers say that crops are mixed in this way because it is too difficult and expensive to separate them. Also, there's no real government pressure in the US for GM crops to be kept separate. As the EU has approved the varieties of GM soya and maize, it can't stop importing mixed crops as the US government claims this would breach international trade agreements.

Most of the maize we eat in the UK is grown in Europe. Genetically-modified maize was grown in Europe last year (mainly in Spain) but it only contributed to a small part of the total maize harvest. The GM variety that is currently grown is mainly used for animal feed.

GM crops in the UK

Field testing and safety assessments must be carried out on each GM crop before consent is given for it to be grown commercially in the UK and approved for use as food. But these controls don't look at the combined effect of growing or eating different GM crops or foods, or at the broader environmental or health consequences.

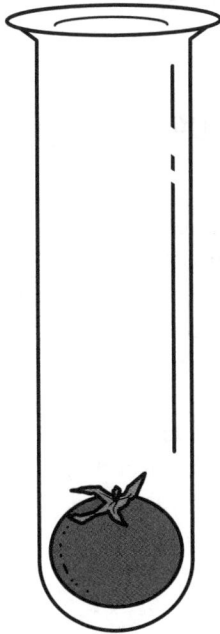

Last year the government announced proposals to tighten the control and look at the wider issues concerning growing GM crops. GM insect-resistant crops can't be grown commercially in the UK for three years and there will be limits on, and monitoring of, herbicide-resistant GM crops for any ecological effects. An industry code of practice and guidelines are being developed to ensure that, when GM crops are grown commercially in the UK, they can be identified and kept separate at all stages from seed through to the final food product. But the problems of monitoring GM crops in the longer-term and ensuring traceability once GM products are in the food chain still need to be tackled.

(Adapted from Which?, *March 1999)*

Document 3:
GM foods – Where do we go from here?

In March 1999, the UK Government announced its new food labelling regulations. All British shops and supermarkets are now required to label clearly foods containing genetically-modified (GM) ingredients such as GM soya and maize as a main ingredient. Also restaurants, cafés, delis, bakers and even hot dog stands are required to inform customers which items contain GM ingredients.

This would be great in theory, but anti-GM pressure groups say that the new law will pressurise small businesses, rather than the biotechnology giants and – as Friends of the Earth stated – 'The reality is that the public will still be eating unlabelled food containing GM ingredients.'

Why? Because the new law excludes genetically-modified food derivatives such as lecithin (from soya) and starch, glucose and dextrose (from maize).

Foods containing these ingredients do not need to be labelled. Emulsifiers found in cakes, bread, chocolate and crisps and vegetable oils are exempt, as is animal feed.

Long-term risks?
As the widespread nature of GM 'contamination' became apparent, public concern over long-term health and safety grew. Gene technology has been around for 20 years, but if we haven't been eating GM foods for more than two or three years, how does anyone know what could happen in the long-term?

The lack of expert opinion has convinced many people of the need for more research into GM foods before it enters the food chain and UK farms.

Tony Blair said there was no scientific evidence to justify a GM ban and doing so would harm 'an important new industry'.

While Prince Charles argued that herbicide
resistant plants would encourage farmers
to use more chemicals and create 'sterile
fields that drive out wildlife'.

The main arguments for GM foods include:

- GM manipulation boosts vitamins and
  lowers the fat content of foods.

- We need to double the world's food
  supply by 2025 and high yielding GM
  crops can help achieve this.

- GM crops can be made drought and
  pest resistant and thus ease famine in
  developing countries.

- Genetic modification is said to produce
  better crop yields, meaning less waste
  and cheaper food.

- GM crops can tolerate spraying with
  a general herbicide while they are
  growing and so need fewer chemicals to
  control weeds, which is better for the
  environment and saves energy because
  of the lower use of farm machinery.

- Stringent regulations are in place to
  test GM foods, so it is unlikely that
  they are harmful.

- Biotechnology has been around for
  thousands of years and our ancestors
  used trial and error to develop different
  crops, domesticate animals and process
  raw foods by brewing, fermentation.

- A by-product of food biotechnology is
  increased knowledge of genetics, which
  benefits science and medicine.

(Adapted from Here's Health, *June 2000)*

Read the three documents on GM food.

Short answer section

1   Using both Documents 2 and 3, synthesise in
   your own words **at least four** of the measures
   that the government is taking to control issues
   surrounding the use of GM (genetically-
   modified) foods.   *(7 marks)*

2   The government is taking various measures to
   control issues surrounding the use of GM foods.
   According to Documents 2 and 3, why are
   these measures viewed by some as inadequate?
   You should consider **two** criticisms from
   each document.   *(6 marks)*

3   Consider the images in Documents 1 and 2.
   How do the images relate to the positive
   and negative messages about GM food
   contained in the documents? For each
   image you should consider **one** positive
   and **one** negative interpretation.   *(6 marks)*

4   Identify **two** key arguments against GM
   food from **each** of the three documents.   *(6 marks)*

Extended answer section

5   You are the press adviser for a consumer group.
   In response to recent public concern about the
   issues surrounding the use of GM products, you
   have been asked to prepare a report based on
   Documents 1, 2 and 3 outlining the long- and
   short-term advantages and disadvantages of
   using genetically-modified products.   *(25 marks)*

Glossary

QCA/CCEA/ACCAC has provided the following glossary of terms used in Key Skills specifications.

Complex – Complex subjects and materials present a number of ideas, some of which may be abstract, very detailed or require you to deal with sensitive issues. The relationship of ideas and lines of reasoning may not be immediately clear. Specialised vocabulary and complicated sentence structures may be used.

Complex activities – The objectives or targets usually need to be agreed with others. Problems will have a number of sub-problems and will be affected by a range of factors. The tasks involved, and the relationship between them, may not be immediately clear. Situations and resources may be unfamiliar.

Complex subjects and materials – Those that include a number of ideas, some of which may be abstract, very detailed or require you to deal with sensitive issues. The relationship of ideas and lines of reasoning may not be immediately clear. Specialised vocabulary and complicated sentence structures may be used.

Critical reflection – This is taken to mean a deliberated process when you take time, within the course of your work, to focus on a period of your performance and think carefully about the thinking that led to particular actions, what happened and what you are learning from the experience, in order to inform what you might do in the future.

Dynamically complex work – Work that includes activities that are inter-related, where it is likely that action in one activity will effect changes in other aspects of the work in ways that may be difficult to predict or control (eg when external changes to timescales or resources produce new problems and you have to balance technical and human demands to meet tight deadlines).

Evidence – What you need to produce to prove you have the skills required. Examples include items you have made, written material, artwork, photographs, audio/video recordings, computer print-outs of text and images, such as graphs and charts, could be used as evidence for written communication and for presenting findings in Application of Number, as well as IT. Records of problem solving activities could include evidence of how you have worked with others, or improved you own learning and performance. Evidence can be used to back up your statements in a progress file or other record of achievement.

Extended documents – Include text books, and reports, articles and essays of more than three pages. They may deal with straightforward or complex subjects and include images such as diagrams, pictures and charts. You are asked to read and write extended documents at Level 2 and above.

Portfolio – A file or folder for collecting and organising evidence for assessment. It should include a contents page to show where evidence for each part of the unit(s) can be found. This may be in hard copy or electronic form.

Problem – There is a problem when there is a need to bridge a gap between a current situation and a desired situation. At Levels 4 and 5, problems will be complex. They will have a number of sub-problems and will be affected by a range of factors, including a significant amount of contradictory information. They will have several possible solutions, requiring you to extend your specialist knowledge of methods and resources and adapt your strategy in working towards a satisfactory outcome.

Objectives – The purposes for working together that are shared by you and other people involved in the activity. Objectives may be those set, for example, by an organisation, your tutor, supervisor or project leader or members of your group or team.

Straightforward – Straightforward subjects and materials are those that you often meet in your work, studies or other activities. Content is put across in a direct way with the main points being easily identified. Usually, sentence structures are simple and you will be familiar with the vocabulary.

Straightforward activities – The objectives, targets or problems are given, or easily identified. It is clear how to break down the work into manageable tasks. Situations and resources are usually familiar.

Substantial activity – An activity that includes a number of related tasks, where the results of one task will affect the carrying out of the others. For example, in Application of Number a substantial activity will involve obtaining and interpreting information, using this information when carrying out calculations and explaining how the results of your calculations meet the purpose of the activity.

Strategy – A plan, for an extended period of time, that builds on what you know from past experiences and includes the development of logical steps towards achieving a specific purpose, but also has scope to adapt approach in response to feedback from others and demands resulting from changes in the wider context of your work.

Targets – The steps for helping you to achieve your personal learning or career goals. Targets should be SMART:
- **Specific** – Say exactly what you need to.
- **Measurable** – Say how you will prove you have met them.
- **Achievable** – Be challenging, but not too difficult for you.
- **Realistic** – Have opportunities and resources for meeting them.
- **Time-bound** – Include deadlines.

Useful Web sites

Key Skills Support Programme
http://www.keyskillssupport.net/

QCA Web sites
Key Skills general information
http://www.qca.org.uk/nq/ks/
Key Skills specifications
http://www.qca.org.uk/nq/ks/main2.asp
Key Skills awarding bodies
http://www.qca.org.uk/nq/ks/keyskills_ab.asp
Level 3 example tests
http://www.qca.org.uk/nq/ks/example_tests_index_3.asp

Exam boards and awarding bodies
The following Web addresses are the specific pages in each exam board/awarding body dedicated to guidance and support for Key Skills.

AQA (Assessment and Qualifications Alliance)
http://www.aqa.org.uk/qual/keyskills.html
Edexcel
http://www.edexcel.org.uk/edexcel/subjects.nsf/
(httpKeySkillsHomePage)?OpenForm
OCR (Oxford Cambridge and RSA Examinations)
http://www.ocr.org.uk/schemes/keyskills/ksindex.htm
WJEC (Welsh Joint Education Committee)
http://www.wjec.co.uk/keyskills.html

CCEA (Northern Ireland Council for the Curriculum, Examinations and Assessment)

http://www.ccea.org.uk/keyskills.htm

ASDAN (Award Scheme Development and Accreditation Network)

http://www.asdan.co.uk/

(Click on 'Key Skills' on the left-hand side menu.)

City & Guilds

http://www.key-skills.org/

Organisations

DfES (Department for Education and Skills)

http://www.dfes.gov.uk/

LSC (Learning and Skills Council)

http://www.lsc.gov.uk/

UCAS (Universities and Colleges Admission Service)

http://www.ucas.ac.uk/

Resources

BBC Education: FE Key Skills

http://www.bbc.co.uk/education/archive/fe/skills/index.shtml

(This site is out of date but offers some useful exercises.)

South Yorkshire Key Skills Passport

http://www.sykeyskills.co.uk/